Contemporary Studies in Literature

Eugene Ehrlich, *Columbia University*
Daniel Murphy, *City University of New York*
  Series Editors

Geoffrey Chaucer

a collection of original articles edited by George D. Economou

McGraw-Hill Book Company

New York • St. Louis • San Francisco • Auckland • Düsseldorf • Johannesburg
Kuala Lumpur • London • Mexico • Montreal • New Delhi • Panama • Paris
São Paulo • Singapore • Sydney • Tokyo • Toronto

123456789 MUMU 798765

Library of Congress Cataloging in Publication Data

Main entry under title:

Geoffrey Chaucer: a collection of criticism.

  (Contemporary studies in literature)
  Bibliography: p.
  1. Chaucer, Geoffrey, d. 1400—Criticism and
  interpretation—Addresses, essays, lectures.
  I. Economou, George D.
  PR1924.G36   821'.1   75-23175
  ISBN 0-07-018968-4 pbk.

In memory of
Elliott Van Kirk Dobbie

Preface

More criticism in a variety of forms has been published about Chaucer's poetry during the last few years than during any previous time—or so it seems to one who has tried to keep up with its constant flow from all of the continents. There are Chaucerians in Africa, Asia, and Australia as well as in this country, Canada, Britain, and continental Europe, and many of them are engaged in extremely important research and thought on our poet. Certainly, Chaucer has joined the select company of poets who belong to the world.

It should not have been very difficult, therefore, to select a number of studies of Chaucer to be reprinted for the first time in a volume for this series. But while almost any such study is quite accessible physically to the student who really cares to find it, often it may not be very accessible intellectually. The undergraduate exposed, perhaps for the first time, to Chaucer's poetry may well find an excellent study that has been written for an audience of scholars to be too difficult, too specialized for the needs of his or her first fascinated reading. Regarding such students as a large and significant contingent of this book's potential audience, I have chosen, rather, to solicit original essays from teachers who are also scholars of Chaucer. We have written what are basically pedagogical rather than scholarly essays through approach rather than through the diminution of our scholarship, the soundness of which I believe will be apparent to Chaucer teachers and specialists, for they—at their various stages of education—are also part of our audience. These audiences are not really mutually exclusive in their requirements or abilities. Indeed, some of these essays make valuable and original points about Chaucer's poetry—a quality encouraged rather than discouraged by their occasion and form.

The contributors, Robert W. Hanning (Columbia), Emerson Brown, Jr. (Vanderbilt), Esther C. Quinn (Hunter), Winthrop Wetherbee (Cornell), Hope Phyllis Weissman (Wesleyan), Elizabeth D. Kirk

(Brown), and Stavros Deligiorgis (Iowa), were invited to write for this collection on the expectation that their known interests in Chaucer and medieval literature would provide appropriately stimulating and authoritative responses to the demands of their subjects. The essays focus largely on the *Canterbury Tales,* but the earlier works are also discussed. Some of us have used footnotes, and others have preferred to append bibliographic notes to our essays. All line references to the works of Chaucer are based on the Robinson edition but without reference to manuscript groups or fragments. We have also adopted Robinson's abbreviations for Chaucer's works, but, for our younger readers' convenience, we have spelled out the complete titles of scholarly journals. The Selected Bibliography is intended not only as an aid for the beginning student but also as a general acknowledgment of the authors' indebtedness to previous scholarship.

Finally, the authors or compilers of all books, but especially of collaborative works, rely on the good offices of many individuals to see them through their tasks. I must therefore thank my wife, Rochelle, and my friends and fellow medievalists Frederick Goldin and Robert Hanning for their consideration, encouragement, and good judgment.

George D. Economou

New York City
September, 1975

Contents

Chronology of Chaucer's Life

Edward III
(1327–77)

1340–45: Born to John and Agnes Chaucer.

1360–98: Served in various military, diplomatic, and unknown missions to France, Spain, and Italy. The 1372–73 and 1378 trips to Italy are considered the most important.

1366–87: Married to Philippa (Roet?), *domicella* of the queen's chamber. They had two sons, Thomas and Lewis, and possibly a daughter named Elizabeth. Philippa died in 1387.

Richard II
(1377–99)

1374–86: Controller in the Port of London.

1386: Knight of the Shire for Kent.

1389–91: Clerk of the King's Works.

1390: Commissioner of Walls and Ditches. Appointed sub-forester of North Petherton Park.

Henry IV
(1399–1413)

1400: Died on October 25, and was buried in Westminister Abbey.

Chronology of Chaucer's Works

Before 1370: Shared in translation of the *Romance of the Rose*.

1368–70: The *Book of the Duchess*.

1372–80: The *House of Fame, Saint Cecilia (Second Nun's Tale)*, and various short poems and lyrics.

1380–86: The *Parliament of Fowls*, translation of Boethius's *Consolation of Philosophy, Palamon and Arcite (Knight's Tale), Troilus and Criseyde*, the *Legend of Good Women*, and various lyrics.

1387–1400: The *Canterbury Tales*.

George D. Economou

Introduction: Chaucer the Innovator

Experiment and innovation in poetry are considerations that are generally raised more urgently in discussions of the works of modern authors than of those of the past. It is very important for us—at least for those among us whose love of literature extends to the contemporary—that we understand the ways in which twentieth-century poets, like Pound and Williams for example, are original and unique, that we recognize as precisely as possible their achievements and influence upon subsequent poetry. This is so, not because the poetry of the twentieth century holds an exclusive patent on innovation, but because the ability to discriminate and define the qualities that make a poet singular, much less great, is an essential part of our discipline: does he "make it new," to use Pound's phrase, and how does he make it new? It is a serious and difficult task, which seems, in many ways to be the more necessary the closer in time and culture the poet stands to us. To generalize conversely, the less contemporary a poet is to us, the more obligated we feel to educate ourselves into a position from which we can make meaningful judgments about his work. In short, what we lack in contemporaneity must be compensated for—by scholarship and informed criticism.

If the quantity of literature about the poetry of Geoffrey Chaucer is any indication, he is a poet whom scholars, teachers, and other poets have deemed worthy of much attention. Having recognized, however diversely, the privilege it is to read and to try to hear him, a community of various kinds of readers reaching back at least to the nineteenth century has committed itself to establishing his text, to developing a proficiency in his language, to perceiving the relationship between his works and their sources, and to investigating the literary, intellectual, social, and historical milieu in which he lived and wrote. In effect, a massive amount of scholarship and a lot of brainpower have been expended in the cause of improving our situations as his readers. One result has been an increasing awareness of something that has been generally recognized for a long time: Chaucer was a most original and inventive poet, whose innovations and vision have affected the course of poetry both technically and thematically down to the present day. The more we learn about the medieval period—the more we learn about literature before and after him—the better we understand his genius and his influence.

Because he is a major poet, there has been considerable interest in Chaucer's life. Biographical data have certainly proven useful in establishing a chronology for his work, but have had a slight effect, in the long run, on interpretation of the poetry. One of the earliest approaches to his work, which still has a few advocates, attempts to discover a historical and political context for passages and for entire works, especially the *Book of the Duchess* and the *Parliament of Fowls,* with the purpose of identifying specific occasions or historical persons as essential elements. Although the kind of historical allegory that arises from this approach is not very interesting to most critics and teachers today, we must remain open to the possible relevance of fresh historical discoveries to our perspective of his career.[1]

The fact of the matter is that Chaucer does not make very many explicit references to historical events or persons. This should trouble us no more than the fact that among the numerous life-records—493 are listed in the chronological table (1357–1400) appended to the standard collection of this material—not a single one identifies Chaucer the civil servant, courtier, diplomat, and private citizen, who had his share of legal and financial problems, with the Chaucer we are all really interested in—the poet. Still there is no reason why we should seriously doubt they are one and the same man, particularly since other kinds of evidence link them. The absence of the identification of Chaucer ''as poet'' in the records hardly denies such a fact; the records by and large show a man of considerable reputation and importance, especially in the world of government service. Reference to his activity or reputation as poet would have been irrelevant. There are stories about colleagues of Wallace Stevens in the insurance pro-

---

[1]See, for example, John N. Palmer, ''The Historical Context of the *Book of the Duchess:* A Revision,'' *The Chaucer Review,* 8 (1974), 253–61.

fession who didn't have the slightest notion he was a poet. And how many of Dr. William Carlos Williams' patients or medical associates knew or cared about his commitment to poetry? So Chaucer the man of affairs is necessarily a shadow and of minimal interest to most of us, but Chaucer the poet engages us more and more. It is as if the perimeter of the famous manuscript illumination of him reading to a noble audience (Corpus Christi College, Cambridge, MS 61) has expanded to include us along with all of his earlier readers, for we are the latest in a series of generations who have become his avid audience.

Because we are part of this continuity of readers, it might be a good idea to review—if only quickly—the achievements of our predecessors so that we can better define our own responsibilities.

Every time we open our editions of Chaucer, we stand indebted to the painstaking and often brilliant linguistic and textual work that has made it possible for us to read him without being overwhelmed by problems many of us are hardly aware of. The work of scholars and editors like Furnivall, Skeat, Manly and Rickert, Robinson, and Baugh, to name a few, has placed poetry written over five hundred years ago in our hands—from manuscript and early printing to our text editions—with all the aids necessary for confident and undeflected reading. Like the other editors of classical and medieval texts, these individuals have made the language and the work accessible to us, and we should recall our dependence, especially whenever we begin to feel superior in all our sophistication to earlier students of literature.

If the major editorial work begun in the late nineteenth century was a response to a scholarly priority, so too was (and still is) the work on Chaucer's sources. The identification of sources and analogues to his poems and the careful examination of their relationships is an extremely complex process that requires careful judgment and wide learning. Source study provides valuable information for the serious Chaucerian regardless of approach. No conscientious scholar should want to write on the *Nun's Priest's Tale,* for example, without first consulting the thorough work on its Old French sources done by Robert A. Pratt, to name a recent study of this nature.[2] Yet pure source studies only remain an important means to the end of informed interpretation, and, like the biographical approach, with which it overlaps in some of its concerns, it does not ultimately satisfy the need to know Chaucer most of his readers feel. The division of the poet's career into

[2]Robert A. Pratt, "Three Old French Sources of the Nonnes Preestes Tale," *Speculum,* 47 (1972), Part I, 422–44; Part 2, 646–68.

French, Italian, and English periods—a practice that is still observed, if only perfunctorily—connects his diplomatic and civil service with his artistic and intellectual growth. While no one would deny that life experience contributes to the development of an artist, it is dangerous to accept the deceptively simple and arbitrary suggestion that Chaucer had to travel to certain countries in order to become familiar with their literatures. According to this scheme, the *Parliament of Fowls* is a poem that should be classified in the "Italian Period" presumably because it was written after the two trips to Italy and because of the adaptation in it of some passages from Boccaccio. Yet Chaucer makes more important use of Latin and French works in what is intellectually his most complex poem up to that point in his career. And *Troilus and Criseyde,* though based on Boccaccio's *Il Filostrato,* may be more profitably approached as a poem in which Chaucer pushed beyond the received limits of the conventional courtly romance by successfully integrating in it his growing powers of characterization and his mastery of philosophical and mythographic traditions with a unique artistic self-consciousness and a highly original perspective of the significance of human and divine history for poetry. As for the *Canterbury Tales* of the so-called English Period, they are no more or less "English" than the *Book of the Duchess* or the *House of Fame*. It is more a question of the difference between early and mature work than it is one of periods of influence. Despite his ingenious and copious use of classical and continental literary traditions throughout his career, Chaucer always remains very much his own man.

The literary criticism that was produced with the early textual and source work on Chaucer often appears to contemporary students to be severely limited, and sometimes it is. This is partly so because the scholarly context of this criticism was narrower and thinner than our own, which, in fact, some of these same individuals were in the process of providing for us. But at times—as we shall see illustrated later—the view of Chaucer's poetry was hampered by extraliterary biases and sensitivities which simply eliminated any possible appreciation of what he had accomplished in a number of the *Tales*. Yet we ought not deceive ourselves into thinking that an early concern such as Chaucer's literary relationships on the level of his sources is a closed book, or that source criticism is a thing of the past. A new study like Jill Mann's *Chaucer and Medieval Estates Satire,* which attempts to show that Chaucer modeled the *General Prologue* in its form and content upon a genre known as estates satire, i.e., "literary treatments of the social classes which allow or encourage a generalised application,'' rather than upon "real life" or society, demonstrates that as critical interpretation of Chaucer is moving in various new directions, some of the old and fundamental questions can still be raised and answered profitably.[3]

Modern Chaucer criticism begins with an approach that can be described as "realist." Whether this approach was stimulated by the currency of realism in the fiction or by the philosophical concerns of the first third of this century—most likely both—is of less importance to us than the help it gives us to understand the development of Chaucer studies in this era. With the establishment of the basic literary context of the work, scholars and critics began to look to "real life" as recorded in historical documents and to their understanding of novelistic fiction in order to deal with what every reader recognizes is one of Chaucer's great strengths as a narrative poet, his art of characterization. It can be remarked that modern Shakespearean criticism opens with A. C. Bradley's character-oriented reading of the tragedies; without pressing the analogy too far, a similar claim can be made for the work of J. M. Manly and George Lyman Kittredge on Chaucer. Manly attempted to show that the Canterbury pilgrims were based upon actual historical persons or composites of persons and that Chaucer was, therefore, applying his ability to observe human nature and society directly to his use of literary forms. Kittredge, on the other hand, was primarily interested in exploring the depth and complexity of Chaucer's characterizations and their interaction. His analyses of Troilus, Criseyde, and Pandarus, which are profoundly but not completely controlled by his famous statement that the *Troilus* is "the first novel, in the modern sense," and his study of Harry Bailly and the Pardoner illustrate the singularity and subtlety of his insights. But his proposal that the prologues and tales of the Wife of Bath, the Clerk, the Merchant, and the Franklin form a unified debate on the question of marriage is perhaps the best known single topic in all Chaucer criticism. It is, in a sense, the epitome of Kittredge's method and contribution, for critics ever since have been compelled to support, repudiate, augment, or revise the concept of the Marriage Group.[4]

[3]Jill Mann, *Chaucer and Medieval Estates Satire* (Cambridge: at the University Press, 1973). The quotation is from page 3.

[4]See George Lyman Kittredge, *Chaucer and His Poetry* (Cambridge, Mass.: Harvard University Press, 1956); and J. M. Manly, *Some New Light on Chaucer* (New York: Holt, 1926).

As we have seen, Mann's recent study has been intended in part as a corrective to the real-life approach to the *General Prologue*.[5] The study of the connections between a work of literature and historical persons and situations can contribute somewhat towards our understanding of that work, but it cannot compete with methods that are more directly involved with the literary and cultural nature of the work. Similarly, critical analysis that relies strongly upon the accepted sense of current literary practice can be restrictive if not at times misleading. Of course, we are also subject to this condition, and our own responses to a literary text are influenced by the creative, critical, and theoretical writing of our time as well as by the work of previous generations. There would be no interest or dynamism to the study of literature if any generation were prepared to concede someone had written the last word on a poem. We cannot be expected to do so for the past, and we cannot expect the future to do so for us.

For the last thirty years, Chaucer criticism, along with literary criticism in general, has been dominated by "historicism" and "new criticism." I use these terms in their broadest rather than in their narrow, doctrinaire senses. By "historicism" I mean an approach that seeks to illuminate the work of art by applying to our interpretation of it as much relevant information as is available about the original period of the work—its social, political, artistic, intellectual, and religious conventions and traditions. By "new criticism" I refer to the commitment of the individual reader to study the text of a poem as an end in itself, bringing to that reading experience for possible application all of his or her knowledge of language and life. Obviously, these two approaches can and have clashed, but for the most part they have proven complementary. Most Chaucer criticism today derives from a frame of reference that consists of a balance of these two approaches. One could argue that the work of Manly and Kittredge and their immediate students fits into or, rather, actually helped develop this frame of reference.

Detailed analysis of Chaucer's poetry in such a historical context has yielded a good number of valuable studies, such as Walter Clyde Curry's investigation of Chaucer's use of various medieval sciences; Charles Muscatine's attempt to trace the development of the major medieval literary styles, the courtly and the bourgeois, and to examine their juxtaposition by Chaucer; or

[5]Mann's book is also a more tacit response to the view of D. W. Robertson, Jr., that the portraits of the Canterbury pilgrims are developed by "iconographic details which point towards an abstract reality." See Robertson's *A Preface to Chaucer* (Princeton: Princeton University Press, 1962), pp. 242–48.

Robert O. Payne's effort to understand the poetry in terms of the "rhetorical poetic" of the Middle Ages, to name only three.[6] The current strong interest in the relationship between literature and the other arts, particularly the fine arts, can be seen as the result of the pervasiveness of the historical method in humanistic studies. This is even true for the revival of interest in "hermeneutics"—neatly defined recently "as the art of rediscovering the authentic thought of the author"—despite the tendency of many writers to treat the subject as if it were more a branch of philosophical than literary study.[7] And finally, the burgeoning of interdisciplinary studies in the medieval period is itself an indication of the continuing liveliness and productivity of historicism in this comprehensive sense.

But historicism's role in Chaucer criticism should not be misconceived as merrily monolithic. There are different kinds of historical method, or, to put it more specifically, there have been radically different ways of understanding and applying historical research in literary criticism. One example, using three eminent Chaucerians and medievalists, should suffice to indicate this. D. W. Robertson, Jr., whose work on Chaucer and other medieval poets has been erroneously singled out (or attacked or promulgated) as being *the* historical criticism, has done as much as anyone to advance its cause with great erudition and dedication. But his weighted view of the significance of the writings of the Church Fathers for the understanding of much later literature and his insistence that medieval literary theory was exclusively an Augustinian one according to which poetry was written and interpreted with the single aim of promoting charity or putting down cupidity, have provoked a serious and productive debate.[8] Equally learned, Morton W. Bloomfield has brought a wide in-

[6]See Walter Clyde Curry, *Chaucer and the Mediaeval Sciences*, 2d ed. (New York: Barnes & Noble, 1960); Charles Muscatine, *Chaucer and the French Tradition* (Berkeley and Los Angeles: University of California Press, 1957); and Robert O. Payne, *The Key of Remembrance* (New Haven and London: Yale University Press for the University of Cincinnati, 1963).

[7]Jean Starobinski, "On the Fundamental Gestures of Criticism," *New Literary History*, 5 (1974), 506.

[8]A useful perspective on the "Robertsonian" controversy can be gained from A. Leigh DeNeef, "Robertson and the Critics," *The Chaucer Review*, 2 (1968), 205–34. Also helpful are the review article of *A Preface to Chaucer* by R. E. Kaske, "Chaucer and Medieval Allegory," *ELH, A Journal of English Literary History*, 30 (1963), 175–92; and "Patristic Exegesis in the Criticism of Medieval Literature: 'The Opposition' by E. Talbot Donaldson, 'The Defense' by R. E. Kaske, and 'Summation' by Charles Donohue," in *Critical Approaches to Medieval Literature*, Dorothy Bethurum, ed. (New York: Columbia University Press, 1960), pp. 1–82.

terest in the history of ideas and literary theory to his reading of Chaucerian texts. His criticism has been particularly helpful to those who wish to further their understanding of medieval literary genres and modes, especially allegory, of Chaucer's own sense of history, as well as of specific ideas associated with the period. And E. Talbot Donaldson, who on first sight appears to write almost as a new critic, combines his critical perceptiveness with philological and textual expertise to reveal aspects of Chaucer's poetry very few could see on their own; for the text and language of a medieval poet are ultimately historical elements that require authoritative handling. In addition to his work on such matters as Chaucer's idiom, Donaldson has made one of the earliest and most compelling cases for interpreting Chaucer the pilgrim-narrator of the *Canterbury Tales* as a persona of Chaucer the poet.[9]

The historical-critical approach to Chaucer continues to flourish at the same time as interest in the poet motivates the application of new methods to his study. This can be illustrated by the concurrent publication of a book like J. A. Burrow's *Ricardian Poetry,* in which the stylistic and thematic common grounds shared by Chaucer and his English contemporaries are explored, and a number of articles in which the principles of the new literary "structuralism" have been applied to the poetry.[10] Even the subject of Chaucer's originality, which I have suggested earlier has always been a special one for Chaucerians, has shown signs of fresh recognitions. Without minimizing all the other attention his work has deservedly drawn, for the remainder of this essay I would like to pursue his poetic innovation in a specific area.

While most criticism of the *Canterbury Tales* inevitably sheds light on Chaucer's uniqueness, it could be argued that since the publication in 1932 of Germaine Dempster's *Dramatic Irony in Chaucer,* studies of the fabliaux have done as much to measure Chaucer's artistic individuality as those of any other specific genre represented in the collection. Before that, the tales of the

[9]See the collections of essays by these two critics: Morton W. Bloomfield, *Essays and Explorations* (Cambridge, Mass.: Harvard University Press, 1970); and E. Talbot Donaldson, *Speaking of Chaucer* (New York: Norton, 1972).

[10]See J. A. Burrow, *Ricardian Poetry* (New Haven: Yale University Press, 1971); Stavros Deligiorgis, "Structuralism and the Study of Poetry: A Paramametric Analysis of Chaucer's 'Shipman's Tale' and 'Parlement of Foules,' " *Neuphilologische Mitteilungen,* 70 (1969), 297–306; and Frederick Turner, "A Structuralist Analysis of the *Knight's Tale,*" *The Chaucer Review,* 8 (1974) 279–96.

Miller, Reeve, Shipman, and Merchant (less importantly, those
of the Friar and Summoner) were fairly ignored in publications
and often in the classroom and lecture-hall as well. Typical of the
uneasiness they caused in the nineteenth century is this bit of
advice in 1854 from the poet Arthur Hugh Clough to F. J. Child
concerning the latter's proposed but finally abandoned plan to
prepare an edition of Chaucer:

> I don't quite see what you should do about the Miller's and Reeve's
> Tales. I think explanation might be a little retrenched there, so as to
> leave them in the "decent obscurity of a learned language."[11]

The idea of holding back scholarly information out of a sense of de-
cency may strike the contemporary reader as odd (ridiculous, if
he is intolerant), but fifty years later in one of those popular
retellings of the *Tales*—to which the eminent Chaucerian F. J.
Furnivall supplied the introduction—the *Miller's Tale* is patheti-
cally reduced to this paragraph:

> This carpenter, so the story said, was persuaded by a clerk that
> there would be second great flood, and that if he wished to be safe
> from drowning he must make himself an ark. So he used his
> kneading-trough as a sort of boat, and was hoisted in it up to the
> ceiling of the kitchen. When the water began to rise, the clerk told
> him he was to cut the cords that held the ark, and drop into the
> flood, and sail safely away. He did exactly as he was told, and for a
> little while hung quietly up in the air, close to the roof, waiting for
> the deluge in a state of great fear and wonder. Suddenly he heard
> someone crying, "Water!" He cut the cords, thinking that the flood
> had come, and down he fell to the hard floor, breaking his arm, and
> getting nothing but laughter for his folly.[12]

This is an extreme case, but it helps us recall the mores of a time
when major Chaucerians like Kittredge and Root, and even some
of a later generation, could hang back from these tales if they
didn't openly disapprove of them. But the pendulum has swung
back, and many critics currently propose that Chaucer's fabliaux

[11]Caroline F. E. Spurgeon, *Five Hundred Years of Chaucer Criticism and
Allusion 1357–1900,* 3 vols. (Cambridge: at the University Press, 1925), vol. 2,
Part 3, p. 17.

[12]F. J. Harvey Darton, *Tales of the Canterbury Pilgrims, Retold from
Chaucer and Others* (New York: Stokes, 1904), p. 54. If such retellings constitute
one of the sins of the past, the numerous modernizations and "translations" that
Chaucerians continue to be tempted into doing constitute a sin that is still very
much with us.

represent his highest art—though lately there are signs of a move towards seeing them as intended by Chaucer to be less serious and more strictly meant to entertain than his other work.[13]

These fabliaux, of which the Miller's and Reeve's will concern me here, and every other tale in the collection have been rightly viewed as a representation in the aggregate of the major genres of medieval literature, just as the gallery of pilgrims depicts a fairly representative picture of the estates and types of fourteenth-century English society. But what is especially remarkable about the organization of the *Tales* is the pairing of the various pilgrims with various types of stories. This brilliant move is one of several important innovations Chaucer made in his conception and execution of the poem. These innovations, we should remember, even as we discuss them singly, are not mutually exclusive but unified in their roles in the poem's entire structure.

Chaucer's pairing of pilgrim and tale has far-reaching implications for a proper appreciation of the work. First, it is a completely *new* way of disposing of a variety of stories within a larger narrative frame such as a pilgrimage. Then it leads to the more important question of the appropriateness of the teller to the tale, a concern that has always fascinated students and critics, particularly because it calls into play a dynamic interaction between the pilgrims' descriptions in the *General Prologue,* and further characterizations elsewhere in the poem with the various factors in, and ultimately the effects of, their tales. To take one example, the Pardoner's portrait in the *General Prologue,* his interruption of the Wife of Bath in her prologue, his own prologue (a kind of confessional monologue) and his tale (a kind of sermon), and his quarrel with the Host at the end of his tale, all must be reckoned with if one is going to develop a full understanding of the pilgrim-tale relationship. And thus, the pilgrim-tale relationship, in turn, forces the consideration of the implications of the exchanges among pilgrims along the way. In other words, we must admit the possibility of a level of interpretation that views the various parts and passages of the poem as the elements of a whole that works dramatically, just as we admit the possibility of a level that works allegorically. This fundamental dramatic principle of the *Tales,* which is fairly commonly accepted, al-

[13]See the articles by Glending Olson, "The Medieval Theory of Literature for Refreshment and its Use in the Fabliau Tradition," *Studies in Philology,* 71 (1974), 291–313; and "The *Reeve's Tale* as a Fabliau," *Modern Language Quarterly,* 35 (1974), 219–30.

lows us to react to each tale as if it were the speech of a fictional character at the same time as we read it as an individual narrative poem or prose piece. This double perspective is made possible by the invention of Chaucer the pilgrim-narrator who 'reports" the entire Canterbury event as the persona of Chaucer the poet who has "created" the entire poetic structure and the various narrative elements it contains.[14] Chaucer the poet, thus, must be heard through his narrator, a persona he had been developing since the *Book of the Duchess,* but this narrator expands rather than limits the possibilities of the poem.

Taken separately and compared with its sources and literary type, any Canterbury tale reveals that Chaucer has probed the genre for new possibilities, has experimented with its conventions, and sometimes has utterly transformed it. Naturally, the Chaucerian touch affects individual poems in different ways, but the basic dramatic conception of the *Canterbury Tales* immediately transforms each tale by virtue of casting it as a speech delivered by a particular pilgrim with particular characteristics and motives. Chaucer fulfills the part of the great poet not by inventing new genres but by altering them to suit his singular purposes. When I describe him to my classes as "Chaucer, the destroyer of genres," I am saying that he is that extremely rare kind of artist who knows how to destroy so that he might build something that is uniquely and forever his own.

This has been "a long preamble of a tale"—by design—for I wish to propose that the prologues and tales of the Miller and Reeve should occupy a special place in our view of the poem. First, when we examine their connections with the fabliau tradition, we recognize they depart significantly from that tradition. A genre that flourished mainly in the thirteenth century in France, the fabliau is a short story in verse, concerned usually with sex, that is intended to make its audience laugh. Summarizing the major views of the genre's two greatest students, D. S. Brewer conveys a concise picture of the type:

> Nykrog, while still accepting Bédier's general literary description of the fabliaux realism, impersonality, lack of rhetorical adornment and of characterization, and rapidity of narration, shows very conclusively their predominantly courtly origin, their quality as

[14]For a stimulating discussion of a possible principle of organization of the *Tales,* see Donald R. Howard, "The *Canterbury Tales:* Memory and Form," *ELH, A Journal of English Literary History,* 38 (1971), 319–28.

written poems, and their emphasis on erotic themes, on satire of the bourgeoisie and of certain clergy (e.g., parish-priests).[15]

Apt as they are for French fabliaux, these observations cannot begin to contain the two Chaucerian tales, where characterization starts with types only to develop into specific individuals, where the circumstances of setting are directly relevant to the characters and plot, where the interdependence of character and action is richly exploited, and where bountiful biblical, liturgical, and literary echoes and allusions extend thematic possibilities. Chaucer's fabliaux constantly threaten to break out of their generic mold and do so in startling ways; it is one of the great revelations for every beginning student to explore the relations between the *Miller's Tale* and its sources and analogues.[16]

But Chaucer was not just making the fabliau new. In subsuming every tale, and its literary line with it, in his own special setting of the pilgrimage frame, he was making a completely new, complex, singular major poem, a kind of *summum* not only of his literary heritage but also of his own poetic inventiveness. I do not think there is a better example in the entire work than the *Miller's* and *Reeve's Tales* as they evolve out of the situation after the conclusion of the *Knight's Tale* to show us Chaucer's intense involvement with the effects inherent in his new formal conception. It is quite certain that the *Knight's Tale* was originally written well before Chaucer began work on the *Tales* and that he revised it for the new poem. The *Miller's Tale* and the *Reeve's Tale,* then, might well have been the first tales written for it, but whether or not they were does not really affect the significance of what we find happening in them.

Many readers have observed that the falling of the cut to the Knight so that he might tell the first tale and the subsequent insistence by the Miller that he will "quite the Knyghtes tale" (3127) over the Host's objections constitute a kind of double acknowledgment on Chaucer's part: of the necessity to recognize both the hierarchical order of society and the pattern of experi-

[15]D. S. Brewer, "The Fabliaux," in *A Companion to Chaucer Studies,* Beryl Rowland, ed. (Toronto/New York/London: Oxford University Press, 1968), pp. 249–50.

[16]The standard reference work is *Source and Analogues of Chaucer's Canterbury Tales,* W. F. Bryan and Germaine Dempster, eds. (New York: The Humanities Press, 1958); but accessible to all students is the admirable paperback collection, *The Literary Context of Chaucer's Fabliaux,* Larry D. Benson and Theodore M. Andersson, eds. (Indianapolis and New York: Bobbs-Merrill, 1971).

ence that is made out of the urgings of individual wills in a world that simultaneously strives to follow its ideals and continuously falls short. This second condition gives rise to the Miller-Reeve match, a combination which is dense with details that reveal Chaucer's awareness of the artistic implications of the unique form he had sprung out of several literary traditions.

When the Miller offers to tell his tale, he does so "in Pilates voys" (3124), reminding us of the ranting character of the mystery plays and of the parallel between the dramatic performances on wagons at designated points along a roadway and the present unfolding of a new scene on the pilgrims' road to Canterbury.[17] Later, in the tale, the analogy attracts to the portrait of Absolon the detail that he enjoyed playing and showing off in the role of Herod in the local mystery cycle (3384); but by that point a parodic comparison between the Holy Family and the principals of the tale has been suggested by other details, and this one then begins to contribute to that comparison by reminding us of the vain king who sought to interfere with the design of Providence, Absolon later interfering with the somewhat different designs of Nicholas and Alisoun. Returning to the *Miller's Prologue,* the provoked Reeve's objections to what he considers personal slurs in the Miller's description of the tale he is about to tell initiate a conflict that involves a considerably larger context than that of the immediate narrative moment. First, it returns us to the portraits of these two pilgrims in the *General Prologue,* where the professional and personal bases for their enmity are established. Also, the portraits provide details that turn up later in their tales, from the teasing implications of the facts that the carpenter's boy in the *Miller's Tale* happens to be adept at removing doors (*Gen Prol,* 550; *MillT,* 3466-71) and who, like the Miller himself (*MillT,* 3129), also happens to be named Robin, to the Reeve's description of the miller in his tale in physical terms we have already encountered in the narrator's description of the pilgrim-Miller. The display of anger (among other things) the Reeve makes in his own prologue, which is interrupted by Harry Bailly's first reference to the passage of time and towns (*RvT,* 3905-8), is channeled into the telling of a fabliau tale that closely identifies its victim with the teller's prior tormentor. As in the tales of the Friar and Summoner, Chaucer has invented a miniature "fictional" *roman à clef* situation in which the aggressor, in this case

---

[17]For a detailed discussion of the relationship between the *Miller's Tale* and the mystery cycles, see Beryl Rowland, "The Play of the *Miller's Tale:* A Game within a Game," *The Chaucer Review,* 5 (1970), 140-46.

the Miller, tells a provocative story that may or may not be about the Reeve, who, in return, fires a vindictive story that leaves little, if any, doubt as to the identity of its mark. Thus, Chaucer's larger fiction of the pilgrimage provides not only the occasion but also some of the specifics of the smaller fictions it contains. Each tale is appropriately paired with its teller, but they are well matched as a pair of tales in the social and moral qualities that bind together the two tellers and the characters in their tales.

One could go on at length discussing the novelties in these tales: Absolon's parody of the Song of Songs in the *Miller's Tale,* the student Aleyn's parody of the *aube* (dawn song) in the *Reeve's Tale,* the use in the latter of dialectal features in the speech of the two Cambridge students who hail from "Strother,/Fer in the north" (4014–15), and the masterful art of character portraiture that flows directly out of the *General Prologue* into both tales. And one finally stops, in the expectation that others will pursue the matter for themselves.[18]

Chaucer criticism through the years has in fact dealt primarily with the question of literary "tradition and the individual talent" of Geoffrey Chaucer, to appropriate the phrase, if not the critical imperatives, of T. S. Eliot. For every generation of students has had to confront this very rewarding issue for itself. The essays in this volume represent an effort by a few of the present generation's teachers of Chaucer to commit to print what we have found most significant in our reading, thinking, and talking about Chaucer with each other and our students. Some of our essays approach old questions in what I hope are new and fruitful ways, and others raise what I hope are in some way new questions that will join the older ones to form a useful context for future teachers and scholars. In any case, we must all take heart in the certain knowledge that our poet is greater than the sum of all our interpretive gifts—past, present, and future.

[18]Such an enterprise would be well served by consulting A. C. Baugh, *Chaucer*, A Goldentree Bibliography (New York: Appleton-Century-Crofts, 1968), pp. 70–72. I especially recommend the articles by Paul E. Beichner, E. T. Donaldson, R. E. Kaske, Paul N. Siegel, and Gardiner Stillwell listed there.

Robert W. Hanning

The Theme of Art and Life in Chaucer's Poetry

In the third book of Chaucer's enigmatic dream-poem, the *House of Fame*, the narrator offhandedly mentions a group of "smale harpers" who imitate greater artists like Orpheus and Arion as an ape would, "or as craft [art] countrefeteth kynde [nature]." (1201–3). This casual comparison of art and life states, with characteristic Chaucerian indirection, a concern that runs like a strong and lively current beneath or at the surface of much of Chaucer's poetry: the relationship between the artistic impulse that underlies storytelling, role-playing (the creation of a "false" identity), or the use of language to foster illusion, and the world of experience to which the artist's imagination must always respond. By probing this relationship, Chaucer is of course commenting on the power and limits of his own "craft," but he is also exploring the basic propensity we all share to transform, in fact or in fancy, the reality of our character and our situation, to bring it into line with our desires or felt needs. Nowhere in Chaucer's works, nor perhaps in all of English literature, is the relationship between art and life scrutinized so brilliantly, with such complete recognition of its complexity, as in the *Canterbury Tales*. In creating this collection of abundantly varied short narratives, Chaucer hit upon the idea of creating an equally varied group of characters—"Wel nyne and twenty in a compaignye,/Of sondry folk" (*Gen Prol,* 24–25)—who have in common only two things: "pilgrimes were they alle" (26), and consequently (as we shall see), storytellers were they all as well. This essay will suggest some of the ways in which Chaucer exploited the scheme of the *Canterbury Tales* to enlighten us about the nature of the art he practiced, as well as about the larger topic of "craft's" debt to "kynde"—and vice versa.

Already in his earliest known poem, Chaucer had introduced this topic by creatively manipulating two conventions of medieval courtly narrative: the dream vision and the overt use of an earlier story as source, catalyst, or major ingredient. The *Book of the Duchess,* written in response to the death of Blanche, wife of John of Gaunt, Duke of Lancaster, in 1368, begins with the narrator recounting the terrible effects of his grief-induced eight years' sleeplessness [!]. Immobilized by his "sorwful ymagynacioun," *(BD,* 14), the narrator reads in a book the story of Seys and Alcyone (Ceyx and Alcione), ultimately derived from Ovid's *Metamorphoses,* and soon falls asleep after propitiating Morpheus (a character in the Ovidian tale) with a feather bed. In his dream, he encounters a black knight who grieves for and, pressed by the narrator, tells about, the peerless lady he has loved and lost. The knight's story comes to its inescapable conclusion— "She ys ded!" (1309)—and after the narrator's tonally ambiguous reply, "Be God, hyt ys routhe," (1310), he and the knight part. He awakes, finds his book still in his hand, and, impressed by his "queynt" dream, decides to put it "in ryme" at once. The last line announces the conclusion of dream and poem alike: "This was my sweven; now hit ys doon." (1334)

There is much scholarly disagreement about the intent and meaning of the *Book of the Duchess*, but at one level the poem shows how the sterile, uncreative state of "sorwful ymagynacioun" can be transformed into a "sweven in ryme"— that is, how the debilitating experience of grief can become a poem about grief, a beautiful artifact that can offer consolation and even pleasure to those (like John of Gaunt) who must live with sorrow. The key element in this process of metamorphosed grief is the story of the lost loved one adapted by Chaucer from Ovid, master of poetic metamorphosis. The old tale (which stands for poetic tradition as a whole, and also as an example of art about grief) allows the narrator to create, in his own dream (clearly a metaphor of poetic inspiration), a confrontation with his own sorrow—"For y am sorwe and sorwe ys y" (597)—in the externalized and idealized form of a black knight. By respectfully, but persistently, forcing the knight to speak of his love affair and its lost object, the dreamer in effect calls into being a series of literary forms—a lyric lament (475–86), the extended metaphor of a lost chess game with Fortune (617–86), and an account of meeting and wooing the ideal courtly lady (759f.)—to which he can respond as a sympathetic but detached, and even critical, audience, while the knight, as "poet," must in turn concentrate on problems of clear and accurate presentation. The resultant dream-dialogue, recalled in the waking world, stands in obvious comparison to the Seys-Alcione story of loss and grief; the latter, still present as the book in the narrator's hand, now prompts the last stage of the creative process, as it did the first: the clothing of inspiration in poetic language.

Chaucer's claim, then, seems to be that art itself is the catalyst drawing forth new art from even the most paralyzing experience, perhaps by offering a model for detached response to reality, or perhaps by a more arbitrary and mysterious process. Chaucer complicates this issue by changing the tone and content of his Ovidian exemplar so that it stands in his retelling as a tale of artistic inspiration (Seys prays for a dream from Juno) and power (Morpheus, at Juno's bidding, actually resurrects Alcione's dead body to appear to Seys in her dream); but Seys's vision, called from the sterile, deathlike depths of sleep,[1] is a flat and final announcement of death, paired with consolatory formulas ["Awake! let be your sorwful lyf!" (202)] all uttered by the husband whom she will not see again: "With that hir eyen up she casteth/And saw noght." The effect of such revelation is death: " 'Allas!' quod she for sorwe,/And deyede within the thriddle morwe." (212–15) By omitting the final, death-defeating metamorphosis of Seys and Alcione into birds (Ovid's conclusion), Chaucer completes his creation of a paradigm of negative art, a story of failed consolation and death. Yet this paradigm

---

[1]The cave of Morpheus is placed by Ovid in a fertile, poppy-strewn landscape; Chaucer instead speaks of

> the derke valeye
> That stant bitwixen roches tweye
> Ther never yet grew corn ne gras,
> Ne tre, ne [nothing] that ought was,
> Beste, ne man, he noght elles,
> Save there were a fewe welles
> Came rennynge fro the clyves adoun,
> That made a dedly slepynge soun.　　　　　(*BD*, 155–62)

Chaucer derived hints for his changes from a French love-vision by Machaut and Statius's *Thebaid* (see J. Wimsatt, "The Sources of Chaucer's 'Seys and Alcyone,' " *Medium Aevum*, 36 (1967), 231–41), but the new picture is his own.

prompts a dream of a green world within which two men communicate fruitfully about sorrow and inspire poetry, not death, when the dream ends. In one sense, then, the *Book of the Duchess* argues the poet's power to transform both his sources and his "waking" experience into a revitalizing, purely personal artistic vision;[2] but in another, it argues for meaningful contact between human beings (the dialogue of dreamer and knight), not isolated poetic utterance (Seys's dream, the black knight's lament), as the basis of consolation. No one model adequately defines art's link to life.

Later, in his magnificent long poem, *Troilus and Criseyde,* based on Boccaccio's *Il Filostrato,* Chaucer took up the theme of art and life in a different, but equally striking, manner. In such a brief essay as this, one can do no justice to the *Troilus,* but it is worth noting that the narrator who undertakes to tell the story of Troilus's "double sorwe" in love lacks any experience of love himself. His guide in writing about this most intimate of human experiences will be his "auctor," Lollius, who has told the story in Latin. At the beginning of Book Two, the narrator states the task of an artist such as he is succinctly: "Myn auctor shal I folwen, if I konne." (2.49) Where does experience fit into this closed circuit of art imitating art? It is supplied by the audience, whom the narrator asks on several occasions to fill out his imperfect and insensitive narrative by referring to their own understanding of love. When Troilus and Criseyde are in bed together, he says:

> Of hire delit, or joies oon the leeste,
> Were impossible to my wit to seye;
> But juggeth ye that han ben at the feste
> Of swich gladnesse, if that hem liste pleye!
> ⋯⋯⋯⋯⋯⋯⋯⋯⋯⋯⋯⋯⋯⋯⋯⋯
> For myne wordes, heere and every part,
> I speke hem alle under correccioun
> Of yow that felyng han in loves art,
> And putte it al in youre discrecioun
> To encresse or maken dymynucioun
> Of my langage, and that I yow biseche.   (3.1310–13, 1331–36)

[2]Lines 275–90 of the *Book of the Duchess* claim that the narrator's dream is unique, that even history's famous dream interpreters could not explain it:

> Me mette so ynly swete a sweven,
> So wonderful, that never yit
> Y trowe no man had the wyt
> To konne wel my sweven rede.   (276–79)

As these lines make clear, the narrator is inviting his audience to become poets themselves, and implying by the reference to "loves art" (recalling Ovid's *Ars Amatoria*, a witty guide to love strategy) that success in this area of experience involves gifts analogous to the poet's.

The blurring of lines between art and experience, or poet and audience, occurs elsewhere in *Troilus and Criseyde*. The difficulties of an inexperienced narrator in creating a love story are echoed within his chosen plot. Troilus, the protagonist, is inexperienced in love (thanks to Chaucer's alteration of Boccaccio's poem), and *his* "love story" must be "created" for him by his friend Pandarus, "that wel koude ech a deel/ The old daunce" (3.694–95)—i.e., who was a master of the artful and strategic side of love. When the narrator depicts Pandarus, at the end of Book One, planning to be Troilus's surrogate in wooing Criseyde, he uses the simile of a craftsman planning to build a house—an image borrowed from a thirteenth-century treatise on the proper construction of a poem! The implied parallel between Pandarus and the narrator is strengthened by the fact that Pandarus, too, has no first-hand experience of successful love (see, e.g., 1.621f.) and that he and the narrator both have an emotional involvement with Criseyde quite unwarranted by their status as, respectively, experiential and poetic architects of a love affair.

The effect of these and many other brilliant modifications of *Il Filostrato* by Chaucer is that throughout *Troilus and Criseyde* the love affair and the act of poetic creation become metaphors for each other. In fact, by the end of the poem, "poet" and "hero" have to some extent changed places: the narrator so loves Criseyde that he is reluctant to follow Lollius in condemning her unfaithfulness to Troilus ("Iwis, I wolde excuse hire yet for routhe," 5.1099), while Troilus, waiting for his beloved's promised return to Troy from the Greek camp (a return that never comes), stands on the city walls and transforms reality into lyric love poetry:

> And hardily this wynd, that more and moore
> Thus stoundemele encresseth in my face,
> Is of my ladys depe sikes soore.
> I preve it thus, for in noon othere place
> Of al this town, save onliche in this space,
> Fele I no wynd that sowneth so lik peyne:
> It seyth, 'Allas! whi twynned be we tweyne?'   (5.673–79)

Criseyde's faithlessness mocks both the lover-turned-poet and the poet-turned-lover; both the hero's love affair and the narrator's love story have proven impossible to construct in the way they had wished. Even Pandarus, the successful "artist" of love, who molds experience to fit his vision in the first three books of the poem so that Troilus and Criseyde do consummate their love—even he is forced by experience (Criseyde's departure from Troy in an exchange of prisoners) to change his art in the last two books and attempt to convince Troilus, in the manner of Ovid's *Remedia Amoris,* to forget his beloved and cultivate other women. Chaucer's paradoxical message would appear to be that experience defeats art's attempt to order and control it, yet art and experience are finally mirror images, two versions of the same frustrating reality with which all human beings must grapple.

Chaucer's exploration of the art-life dialectic in the *Canterbury Tales* shows continuities with the *Troilus,* but also happy innovations. His basic change, already mentioned, was to create a narrative frame in which a large cast of disparate characters tell each other stories while pursuing a common enterprise, the pilgrimage to Saint Thomas Becket's shrine in Canterbury that was one of late medieval Christendom's most popular voyages. Manuscript evidence shows that, as Chaucer worked on the *Tales* over a number of years, he repeatedly altered the sequence of stories and the links between them and even, it would seem, reassigned tales to new tellers or created elaborate autobiographical statements to precede them. Such ongoing revision suggests several motives: the desire to give a pilgrim matter appropriate to his character and to develop varied relationships and dramatic rivalries among the pilgrims, reflecting the range of interactions possible when thirty human beings of unique temperament and experience are temporarily thrown together by a common intent.

If the framed and linked story collection appealed to Chaucer as a tool he could use to etch, with mimetic accuracy, life's complex social relationships, it also attracted him as a literary structure offering maximum possibilities to demonstrate artistic virtuosity and control. Within it he could incorporate a wide variety of literary genres—romance, fabliau, saint's legend, sermon, *exemplum,* etc.—adapted to suit his needs. He could also rise to the challenge of getting from one story to the next in the largest number of ways: unobtrusively, raucously, by means of balance or parody, as part of an extended discussion of a theme that spans several tales. Chaucer's inspiration for this latter purpose—the demonstration of mastery—was probably Ovid's *Metamorphoses*, an enormous collection of mythological stories tenuously linked by the theme of change, set into a fifteen-book epic structure, and most frequently concerned to demonstrate the artist's power to create his own, convincing yet clearly artificial vision of reality. In the *House of Fame,* Jove's eagle, when speaking to the narrator, refers to the *Metamorphoses* as "thyn oune book" (712); certainly, the constant metamorphosis of narrative focus as Ovid ingeniously moves from one tale to the next would have appealed to a self-conscious artist like Chaucer, as would the Roman poet's often comic or dramatic application of epic, pathetic, and psychological rhetoric to narratives of men become statues or maidens trees.

The coincidence of expanded mimetic and virtuosic intentions on Chaucer's part gives the *Canterbury Tales* an incredibly ambitious double program: to subordinate art most fully to the manifold experiences of life in order to reproduce them faithfully, and yet to show how art dominates and metamorphoses experience by imposing on it structures that satisfy and harmonize purely aesthetic demands for continuity, variety, and authorial control in a literary narrative. If we compare the *Canterbury Tales* with two other famous late medieval framed story collections, Boccaccio's *Decameron* (which Chaucer seems not to have known) and Gower's *Confessio Amantis* (which he certainly did know and parodies good-naturedly in several of the *Canterbury Tales*), we see at once that for the other two artists the narrative frame was primarily an ordering device: the ten refined and elegant young Florentines who flee the Black Death abroad in the city for an idyllic interval at a country villa are much alike in background and interests, while their storytelling arrangements (ten miles a day for ten days, each day having its own "sovereign" who sets the theme for the day's tales) establish an ordered world of art in opposition to the social chaos, vividly described in the prologue, of plague-torn Florence. Gower's device of a lover's confession to Nature's priest, Genius, who tells tales to illustrate each of the seven deadly sins, is even more strictly and artificially structured. In strongest contrast is Chaucer's agglomeration of characters, who stand out each from the other, and who cram the narrative with life and diffuse energy as they converse, squabble, or just gloriously *exist:* the crooked Pardoner singing happily at the offertory of the Mass; the Friar's eyes that "twynkled in his heed aryght,/ As doon the sterres in the frosty nyght" (*Gen Prol,* 267–68); the pustule-faced Summoner, "of [whose] visage children were aferd" (*Gen Prol,* 628); the Knight, a model of chivalric virtue whose overgarment, stained by the rust of his armor, testifies to his hasty change of roles from mercenary to pilgrim. As John Dryden declared admiringly, "here is God's plenty!"

Chaucer's creation of so much variety of character and his observation of his pilgrims from many perspectives—dress, physical and moral makeup, professional skills, behavior, types of relationship with other pilgrims—seem designed to foil any attempt to impose an overall, schematic ordering principle on the *Canterbury Tales.* Some critics, responding naively to this full deployment of Chaucer's mimetic impulse, have attempted to discover the actual contemporaries who served as models for the poet's portraits, while others have constructed pre-pilgrimage biographies for problematic characters like the Pardoner.[3] A more sophisticated critic, J. Mann, has recently shown how Chaucer avoids fitting the pilgrims squarely into the niches prepared for them (and their vices) in the tradition of medieval satire of the professions, thus creating ambiguities and rendering the characters more individuals than types.[4]

Yet the "estates satire" tradition clearly does, as Mann contends, provide a formal principle for the *Prologue,* inviting us to respond to some pilgrims (the Knight, the Clerk) and pairs (Parson and Ploughman, Summoner and Pardoner) as embodiments of Chaucer's schematized socio-moral vision. In fact, close study of the *Tales* as a whole reveals overwhelming evidence of order in abundant chaos, of careful (though subtle) structures that organize variety to make it a thematic vehicle. Two examples of this evidence must suffice: (1) the debate on sovereignty in marriage, proposed many years ago by G. L. Kittredge as a theme uniting the utterances of Wife of Bath, Clerk, Merchant, and Franklin; (2) the more subtle (perhaps too subtle) analysis of the *General Prologue* by H. F. Brooks that sets out to show how the portraits

[3]See M. Bowden, *A Commentary on the* General Prologue *to the* Canterbury Tales (New York: 1948); following J. M. Manly, *Some New Light on Chaucer* (New York: Holt, 1926; reprint Gloucester, Mass.: P. Smith, 1959) for the first attempt; and G. L. Kittredge, *Chaucer and His Poetry* (Cambridge, Mass.: Harvard University Press, 1915, reprinted 1970), pp. 21–22 and 211–18, for the second.

[4]J. Mann, *Chaucer and Medieval Estates Satire; The Literature of Social Classes and the* General Prologue *to the* Canterbury Tales (Cambridge: the University Press, 1973).

are bound together into myriad arrangements and groupings by the use of similarities and contrasts of estate, appearance, moral stature, etc.[5] This latter example, seeking order in Chaucer's artistic technique rather than in thematic units (such as the marriage group) or doctrinal schemes (such as grouping the pilgrims and their tales according to the seven deadly sins, as some have done), clearly illustrates the extent to which Chaucer's text stimulates our desire to find order in all works of art.

We may say, then, that within the *Canterbury Tales* two opposite, polar impulses are vigorously working: one toward mimetic variety and the illusion of a self-effacing art that reproduces life "as it is," the other toward artistic ordering, on various principles, which shatters the mimetic illusion by making us aware of the artist's power to organize experience for thematic or aesthetic purposes. The art historian E. H. Gombrich describes well the tension between these opposed impulses in visual art; his comments will help us in understanding Chaucer's verbal art as well. He speaks of the "interdependence" between

> *composition* . . . [a term] for all principles of order, and . . . *fidelity to nature* . . . [a term] for the means of representation in contour and depth. Clearly, the more a painting or a statue mirrors natural appearances, the fewer principles of order and symmetry it will automatically exhibit. Conversely, the more ordered a configuration, the less will it be likely to reproduce nature. . . . The kaleidoscope presents an orderly arrangement of elements, most snapshots do not. An increase in naturalism means a decrease in order. It is clear, I think, that most artistic value rests among other things on the exact reconciliation of these conflicting demands. Primitive art, on the whole, is an art of rigid symmetries sacrificing plausibility to a wonderful sense of pattern, while the art of the impressionists went so far in its search for visual truth as to appear almost to discard the principle of order altogether.[6]

Chaucer's achievement in the *Canterbury Tales* was to increase, by some feat of genius, what Gombrich calls naturalism *without* decreasing order, but only diffusing it, in disguise,

[5]H. F. Brooks, *Chaucer's Pilgrims, The Artistic Order of the Portraits in the* Prologue (London: Methuen, 1962).

[6]E. H. Gombrich, "Norm and Form," in *Norm and Form, Studies in the Art of the Renaissance* (London and New York: Phaidon, 1966), p. 94. See also page 95 and related comments in another essay, "Raphael's *Madonna della Sedia*," pp. 74, 76, and 78, on how Raphael balances "two mutually limiting demands—that of lifelikeness and that of arrangement," p. 74.

throughout the work. Chaucer's equivalent of "the exact reconciliation of these conflicting demands" does not appear to be
exact or a reconciliation (as it does, say, in a Raphael Madonna),
but rather a constant coexistence of the two elements in a sometimes mysterious, sometimes ambiguous, always exhilarating
way. In the *Prologue* portraits, the roadside rivalries, and the
succession of stories, art seems at one moment to deny itself in
the face of life's variety—a variety it can but strive to reproduce
faithfully—and at the next to impose significance on life by borrowing and organizing material from literary and intellectual
sources. (The Wife of Bath owes important elements of her un-
forgettable personality to an allegorical figure in *Le Roman de la
Rose,* the moral character of the Pardoner or of the Summoner
conforms to his physical features in ways prescribed by medieval
scientific lore, and so on.) In fact, Chaucer includes in the *General Prologue* two voices—the narrator's and the Host's—that
embody the two impulses he seeks to maximize throughout the
Tales. This self-conscious presentation of a "debate" on art's
role in transcribing experience complements the broad statement
of the art-life theme implicit in the way Chaucer sets the scene for
pilgrimage and storytelling throughout the *Prologue.* A glance at
this larger setting should therefore precede analysis of the more
specific statements of poetic intent.

The *General Prologue* opens with an essentially sexual
image to explain seasonal change:

> Whan that Aprill with his shoures soote
> The droghte of March hath perced to the roote,
> And bathed every veyne in swich licour
> Of which vertu engendred is the flour;

From the piercing liquid of April's showers comes new life, the
flower. Successive images of the wind breathing life into "tendre
croppes" and the young sun racing through the heavens complete
the picture of an inanimate world transformed by vital energy.
Then the poet moves on to subhuman animals (small birds who
sleep with one eye open, "So priketh hem nature in hir corages,"
11), and finally to "folk" whose thirst for extraordinary realms of
experience—"straunge strondes,/ [And] fern halwes, kowthe in
sondry londes" (13–14)—becomes, by its place in an ordered,
ascending sequence, an expression of the life force precisely
analogous to the restlessness of the birds and the renewed fertility
of the earth. (This connection is fascinating in light of the wide-

spread medieval view, descended from Augustine, of the Christian life as a pilgrimage through this world, holding aloof from natural delights for the sake of supernatural delights in the world to come.)

Having established a principle of re-creation at work at all levels of existence in Springtime, the poem proceeds to show how human beings, impelled on pilgrimage "with ful devout corage," (22) order the vital energies in annual resurgence within them. These energies force people out of normal routines into chance *encounters* that they quickly organize into *associations:*

> At nyght was come into that hostelrye
> Wel nyne and twenty in a compaignye,
> Of sondry folk, by aventure yfalle
> In felaweshipe, and pilgrimes were they alle,   (23–27)

Man-the-pilgrim is also man-the-social-being; to join an ad hoc group is to partake in ordering it:

> So hadde I spoken with hem everichon
> That I was of hir felaweship anon,
> And made forward erly for to ryse,
> To take oure wey. . . .   (31–34)

It is within such a suggestive framework of strong impulses precisely ordered that the narrator, appealing to "resoun," proceeds to recount the "condicioun" of each pilgrim, i.e., gives vent to another basic impulse, that of representing life in all its variety, by describing the appearance, behavior, and character of one's fellow human beings. In other words, the *ordering* impulse that creates society anew at the Tabard Inn provides the material for the *representational* impulse of the narrator. When he has finished his descriptions (which, as I have suggested, give the simultaneous impression of reproducing life untouched and of constantly ordering it in accord with a variety of systems and perspectives), he pauses before recording "our viage/ And al the remenant of our pilgrimage," (723–24) to apologize for what he claims will be a complete transcript, deleting no expletives, of all that was said and done by the pilgrims (725–29). His excuse for such absolute fidelity to nature—such complete surrender to the representational impulse—is that it is his task to report stories accurately—if he is not to report them inaccurately! (730–40).

In this naive way, the narrator is making a case for an absolutely representational art—for a photographic realism, in fact. This is at once the statement of a fool (who uses the examples of Christ and Plato to countenance obscenity and diffuseness, 732–34) and a radical manifesto that art must be true to life, not bowdlerized, overly selective, or fictional.[7] A second, briefer apology by the narrator is similarly ambiguous: he excuses by his "short wit" his failure to set the pilgrims "in hir degree" (744), that is, according to strict social order. Short of wit he may be, but surely implicit in his claim to report reality exactly is a rejection of "degree" or social decorum as a governing principle—to paraphrase Gombrich, the more a narrative mirrors natural appearances, the fewer principles of order and symmetry it will automatically exhibit.

This, then, is one of the specific artistic voices of the *Prologue,* espousing the mimetic or representational principle absolutely and rejecting, by both design and the accident of short wit, ordering principles of any kind. The other voice is that of Harry Bailly, Host of the Tabard, who reacts very differently to vernal promptings toward personal adventure ("pilgrimage") and social order ("felaweship"). The Host is introduced as a figure of order, organizing the pilgrims at the dinner table:

> Greet chiere made oure Hoost us everichon,
> And to the soper sette he us anon.
>
> ....
>
> A semely man oure Hooste was withalle
> For to han been a marchal in an halle.   (*Gen Prol,* 747–52)

His language and character make him also a figure of "myrthe" (757, 759, 764, 766, 767, 773, 782). In his speech to the pilgrims after supper, the themes of mirth and order coalesce: he proposes to "doon [them] som confort" if they will be governed by him and assent to his judgment. His scheme is to organize the conversation (and presumably storytelling) they will engage in on the road to and from Canterbury. Each pilgrim will tell two tales outbound, two more homebound; the Host, as "juge and reportour," will presumably decide who has told the best tale and thus earned "a soper at oure aller cost" (799) on the return to the Tabard.

[7]It was, of course, absolutely standard procedure for medieval poets to do what the narrator says he must not—"feyne thyng, or fynde wordes newe"(*Gen Prol,* 736)—even when purporting to reproduce exactly "everich a word" of an earlier story. Chaucer was no exception.

The Host thus clearly embodies Gombrich's pole of order in art. He starts with the observed fact that a human being is a *communicating* and *mirth-seeking* animal:

> And wel I woot, as ye goon by the weye,
> Ye shapen yow to talen and to pleye;
> For trewely, confort ne myrthe is noon
> To ryde by the weye doumb as a stoon. (*Gen Prol,* 771–74)

Given this fact, he sees his job as one of articulating and tightly controlling a structure for this behavior. (He makes it clear that whoever disputes his judgment will pay dearly, 805–6.) This structure will presumably maximize the effectiveness ("myrthe") of artistic expression within clearly defined limits on content (the stories are to be "of aventures that whilom han bifalle," 795), as pilgrim-artists compete for the prize; it will also establish an overall shape for the total work (two tales per person in each direction, or 120 tales in all)[8] and thus assure the constant presence on the pilgrimage of the pleasure that comes from social discourse.

Chaucer introduces ambiguity into this manifesto of artistic order, as he did into the narrator's short-witted claim for artistic representation. After all, the Host's whole scheme is designed to keep the "felaweship" together long enough to give Harry Bailly a nice bit of business at the Tabard at journey's end. Chaucer slyly suggests that the artist's penchant for self-aggrandizement underlies much of the activity by which he imposes special structures on the reality he finds around him.

By creating two artists-in-residence on the Canterbury pilgrimage, Chaucer indicates overtly his own interest (as creator of both his would-be surrogates) in giving fullest rein to the impulses they represent in his own poetry while betraying ironically his awareness of the ambiguities involved in espousing a pure form of either. To espouse fidelity to life as an artistic goal is inevitably to reject restrictions on expression that social and moral conventions always impose. To attempt to shape and judge available material from a single point of view and toward a single end is to

[8]The Host is so commanding a figure of artistic order that he has convinced virtually all subsequent critics that his 120-tale plan was also Chaucer's; it seems to me much more likely that Chaucer puts such an ambitious and neat scheme in the mouth of the order figure precisely because it represents an extreme structural paradigm he may have toyed with but to which he was by no means committed. Such a view accords with the less schematic analysis of Chaucer's intentions offered above, p. 20.

create conditions for conflict within the work of art between the ordering vision and the basic impulses to self-expression on which that vision depends (as the Host depends on the pilgrims' intention to chat on the road to Canterbury). Early in the *Canterbury Tales,* the Host's vision is severely tested, as Chaucer moves toward a higher stage of the debate about art's relationship to life that he initiated in the *Prologue.*

As the pilgrimage begins, the pilgrims are forced, by their acquiescence in the Host's plan, into the role of artists, one by one. By chance or by the Host's connivance (*Gen Prol,* 835–45) the Knight, who is the highest pilgrim in "degree," is chosen to tell the first tale—a long, complex narrative of love and war, friendship and chivalry, fortune and destiny. At its conclusion, the pilgrims call it a "noble story," especially the "gentils," those closest in rank to the Knight. The Host, as judge, announces that things are off to a good start (*Mill Prol,* 3114–15) and, as voice of order, chooses the Monk to tell the next story, "somewhat to quite with the Knyghtes tale" (3119). The Monk is roughly the social peer of the Knight in the ecclesiastical order, and the Host's request that he "quite with" the preceding tale suggests that, in creating his ambulatory anthology, the Host is espousing principles of social decorum and artistic balance—the latter itself a type of decorum, since the Monk's religion and learning will presumably produce a story as "noble" as the Knight's chivalric idealism.

At this point, however, the Miller challenges both the Host's assumptions about artistic order and his authority to impose them:

> The Millere, that for dronken was al pale,
> So that unnethe upon his hors he sat,
> He nolde avalen neither hood ne hat,
> Ne abyde no man for his curteisie,
> But in Pilates voys he gan to crie,
> And swoor, "By armes, and by blood and bones,
> I kan a noble tale for the nones,
> With which I wol now quite the Knyghtes tale."   (3120–27)

Although the Miller reasserts the critical language ("noble tale") and artistic goal ("quite the Knyghtes tale") already before the company, they have clearly undergone a sea-change of irony and parody in his mouth. His eschewing of the basic forms of courtesy challenges social decorum, and since we know from the *Prologue* that "He was a janglere and a goliardeys,/ And that was moost of synne and harlotrye" (560–61), his tale will certainly not accord with the Knight's in tone. In fact, his tale is the English language's most famous dirty story, and it "quites" the Knight's by offering a radically and destructively different view of humanity as an appetitive trickster, not (as for the Knight) an earnest seeker after love and truth. For the Miller, to "quite" means to attack, via parody and scorn, art based on an antithetical view of life.

The Miller's challenge extends to the Host's view of good art arising from the imposition of order on old stories and their tellers. He can control neither his horse (*Mill Prol,* 3121) nor his tongue (or so he claims, 3137–40) because he is drunk. He is a figure of Bacchic release, arguably modeled by Chaucer in this respect on Bacchus's follower, Silenus, who, Ovid tells us, could hardly sit astride his jackass due to his inebriation (*Ars Amatoria,* 1.543–44, cf. *Mill Prol,* 3120–21). As such, he rejects the Host's "Apollonian" attempt to maintain decorum, threatening to break the social bond that, as we have seen, underlies storytelling and holds out to the Host a tangible reward for his organizing efforts at the end of the pilgrimage:

> Oure Hooste saugh that he was dronke of ale,
> And seyde, "Abyd, Robyn, my leeve brother;
> Som bettre man shal telle us first another.
> Abyd, and lat us werken thriftily."
> "By Goddes soule," quod he, "that wol nat I;
> For I wol speke, or elles go my way." (3128–33)

By refusing to give way to "som bettre man" (of higher rank? more sober?), the Miller not only rebuffs the Host's artistic principle; he also presents a new model of art's relationship to life. Art can be the medium of direct response to, and attack upon, people and values (in this case, the Knight and chivalry) with whom life's "aventure" brings one into contact. In one sense, then, the Miller is not simply a disruptive figure; through his intervention, one paradigm—art is order applied to the imagination and social reality in accord with principles of decorum, for the sake of pleasure and profit—gives way to another—art is the sphere in which, released from inhibition by inspiration, the artist can safely tell the truth about existence, no matter how offensive it may be to rival views of life.

The Miller's announcement that he will tell a tale of a cuckolded carpenter arouses the ire of the Reeve, who has practiced that trade and assumes he is the personal target of the bawdy story (3141–49). To avenge himself, he tells the next story, in which a proud miller is cuckolded and badly beaten by two clerics (northerners, like the Reeve himself). He, too, uses art to "quite" a rival (*Rv Prol,* 3864–65), but in his case, he is taking personal vengeance for an insult, and his story provides the satisfaction of wish fulfillment; the *General Prologue* makes it clear that the spindle-shanked Reeve, with his rusty sword, could never hope to treat the Miller in life as his surrogate protagonists treat the Miller's surrogate in his tale. This is, then, yet another statement by a Chaucerian artist-figure of art's relationship to experience: it is a wishful weapon of revenge for the indignities life inflicts on us.

By a final irony, the sequence of tales, Knight-Miller-Reeve, which is at first glance the result not of art's orderly response to life, but of its use as an instrument of disruption and unpremeditated response, is in fact the most closely unified and integrated sequence in the *Canterbury Tales.* "Quyting," Chaucer suggests, for all its spontaneity and indecorousness, its visceral and irrational component, is as good a basis for controlled art as is the Host's fussy planning. At this level, then, Chaucer seems to supply a synthesis for the dialectic statements of art-as-representation and art-as-order in the *General Prologue.*

One further aspect of the *Miller's Prologue* (which is, in a sense, one of the richest quarries of artistic theory in all medieval literature) deserves attention. The narrator, apologizing once again at the end of the *Prologue* for the bawdy tale he is about to report, advises his audience: "And therfore, whoso list it nat yheere,/ Turne over the leef, and chese another tale;/ . . . Blameth nat me if that ye chese amys" (3176–81). Embedded in this doubtfully exculpatory statement is Chaucer's comment on the implications of a major revolution of his time, the formation of a large, middle-class reading public that could afford to collect inexpensive manuscipts, produced in commercial scriptoria.[9] Unlike the court audience to which Chaucer presumably read his poetry aloud (as he is shown doing in a famous illustration from Corpus Christi College Manuscript 61), this new and growing audience encountered the poet via private reading—a circumstance which did indeed allow the reader to "turne over the leef and chese another tale"—that is, to establish his or her

[9]See L. H. Loomis, "Chaucer and the Auchinleck MS," in *Essays and Studies in Honour of Carleton Brown* (London: Oxford University Press, 1940), pp. 111–28; and "The Auchinleck MS and a Possible London Bookshop of 1330–1340," *Publications of the Modern Language Association,* 57 (1942), 595–627.

own order for a work of art and a different one for each reading, if he or she chose. In other words, the technology of literacy had as a side effect the partial obliterating of the line between artist and audience. By choosing what part of a work he or she will read and in what order he or she will read it, the reader usurps part of the poet's function and becomes, in effect, a figure like the Host, ordering art for pleasure or decorum.

Chaucer's playful invitation to his readers (as opposed to his public audience) pulls the readers into the poem, and with them the personal experience and values they bring to the act of readership. We saw Chaucer issue an analogous invitation to his audience in the *Troilus,* but there it involved using experience to complete what art leaves unfinished; here our experience and tastes will truncate the "too complete" work of art to make it palatable. Once again Chaucer denies the existence of a clear boundary between experience and art, by making us confront the artist's ordering principle at work in ourselves. Indeed, in other places in the *Canterbury Tales,* he also invites us to augment his creative impulse by making explicit in our own imaginations connections between characters which the text barely and fleetingly suggests. For example, is Robyn the carpenter's servant in the *Miller's Tale* the same as Robyn the Miller who tells the tale? (Both Robyns are adept at heaving down doors by brute force.) These characters exist at different levels of Chaucer's fiction; one has created the other in his own image, or rather, Chaucer has created both but left the door ajar for us to supply the Miller with a motive for his cameo appearance in his own tale, by using our imaginations. Similarly, a tissue of verbal recalls of the *Miller's Tale* at the moment when the Wife of Bath is describing her fifth husband, a clerk of Oxford, beckons us into a momentary identification of Alisoun of Bath with Alisoun of Oxford, as if the former were an older (and wiser?) but still lusty version of the latter. Full reading of the text makes the identification impossible, of course, but Chaucer, I believe, wants us to go against his text here, to create a more satisfyingly interconnected poetic universe than his own. In short, Chaucer wants us to *feel*, not just to surmise, the process of artistic creation; for what we do to his poem, in ordering or augmenting it from within ourselves, is what he, as artist, is constantly doing to experience in metamorphosing it into a poetic artifact.

Chaucer's interest in exploring the power and the boundaries of art in the *Canterbury Tales* does not confine itself to passages and situations overtly concerned with storytelling. In a variety of

ways, he surveys what can—and cannot—be accomplished by
language, verbal deceit, illusion, role-playing, and other guises
assumed by the artistic impulse when faced with the exigencies of
experience. A glance at a few such instances will complete this
essay. Chaucer anatomizes role-playing in the portraits of the
Prioress and the Pardoner. The Prioress "peyned hire to countrefete cheere/ Of court" (*Gen Prol,* 139–40)—her manners and demeanor, her very name Eglentyne, are those of a court lady.
Denied "femininity" by her vocation and the role it thrusts upon
her, the Prioress responds by imposing a different role on that of
the lady ecclesiast: the delicate and fastidious grand dame who
"leet no morsel from hir lippes falle,/ Ne wette hir fyngres in hir
sauce depe" (128–29). Chaucer makes the limitations of the performance quite clear:

> And Frenssh she spak ful faire and fetisly,
> After the scole of Stratford atte Bowe,
> For Frenssh of Parys was to hire unknowe.   (124–26)

Since, however, "al was conscience and tendre herte" in her
character, we do not know, finally, where role (art) ends and the
"real" Prioress begins. This surely is the point of the portrait's
last touch, the brooch inscribed *Amor vincit omnia:* Is the love
religious or secular? Is this a credo or part of the act? The
Prioress's art of self-presentation cannot finally protect her from
our gentle laughter, but it can and does insulate her against our
attempt to find the real woman behind the mask.

The Pardoner is complicated in a different way. His physical
self-presentation fails abundantly. He imagines himself a dandy in
appearance and demeanor—"Hym thoughte he rood al of the
newe jet" (*Gen Prol,* 682)—but his hair is too thin, his eyes glare
like a hare's, and his small voice and lack of facial hair betray
sexual incompleteness: "I trowe he were a geldyng or a mare,"
(691). His moral failure is as complete as the physical and sarto-
rial; he wins money duping the ignorant with false relics. And yet,
this threefold insufficiency coexists with enormous verbal ac-
complishment in the pursuit of iniquity: "But of his *craft,* fro
Berwyk into Ware,/ Ne was ther swich another pardoner . . ."
(692–93) [italics mine]. By his morally bankrupt artistry, he makes
more in one day than an honest parson in two months. Chaucer
thus raises, in characteristically extreme form, the question of
whether art need have a moral base in experience to succeed, and
he seems to answer in the negative. The juxtaposition in the *Prologue* of the Pardoner's deceitful virtuosity and the narrator's

apologetic claim to be completely truthful and self-effacing ·in reporting *everything* the pilgrims said constitutes a typically Chaucerian ambiguous statement about art and truth.

The question of art's power and limits is raised self-consciously in Part Three of the *Knight's Tale*. This section describes in great detail three temples built by Theseus, Duke of Athens, as part of the lists he has ordained as the setting for the battle between Palamon and Arcite for the hand of Emelye. (The lists are on the same spot where Theseus found the two knights fighting to the death for the same reason, but without his permission or the restraining rules he will lay down for the tournament.) Theseus hires the best artists to "devyse" the temples, with their statues and paintings (1897–1901), and the Knight sets himself in artistic rivalry with these masters when he undertakes to "devyse" (describe) them himself (1914–17). The description of each temple is an evocation of that part of human activity and fortune governed by each respective deity: Mars, Venus, Diana. What interests Chaucer is the way the artist can reduce areas of pain and chaos in actual experience (for each temple is an anthology of suffering and disaster) to beautiful, self-contained artifacts; that is, how he or she can construct his or her own alternative reality. We see this especially clearly in the temple of Mars (1967f.), where the process of metamorphosis from life to art is underscored by a triple *ecphrasis*, or description of a work of art: within the actual temple is a wall painted to resemble the temple of Mars in "Trace"—but the painting is that of a forest landscape with a temple standing within it, and within *that* painted temple are the scenes which the Knight not only describes but which he says, "ther I *saugh*." (1995) [italics mine] That is, the Knight looks directly at the paintings he has created in his mind; the distance in time and space between himself on the road to Canterbury and the temple outside ancient Athens is obliterated—as is the normal sensory limitation of visual art, for the Knight not only sees but hears things happening in his imagined world (1979–80, 2004, 2011). And yet this freezing of reality into superb images by the Knight, like the creation of a controlled setting for the fury of Palamon and Arcite by Theseus, which setting the Knight is ostensibly describing, cannot in fact order experience to accord with human desire. Arcite wins the tournament, but as he rides about the lists in triumph, he is struck from his horse and killed by the intervention of Saturn, who snuffs out the victor's life, irrespective of justice, in order to keep peace among the other gods. In the face of such amoral power, the artist's power in creating images of order seems somehow irrelevant—perhaps even a cruel hoax.

The *Franklin's Tale* also solicits difficult questions from us about art's response to harsh facts of life. The tale abounds in images of art: the dance, the cultivated garden, and, above all, magic. Aurelius, the genteel squire who loves Dorigen, is told by her to remove the "grisly rokkes blake" that threaten her beloved husband's homecoming, if he would win her favor. In desperation, he pays a cleric of Orleans 1,000 pounds to make the rocks *seem* to disappear for a week or two by means of magic.[10] The cleric entertains Aurelius in his house by creating brief, illusory scenes of hunting, of chivalry, and of himself dancing with Dorigen. The location of this seance "in his studie, ther as his bookes be," (1207) and the impermanence of the effect ("he clapte his handes two,/And farewel! al oure revel was ago," 1203–4) suggest that the cleric is at least distantly comparable to the Knight as a creator of a temporary, alternative world of beauty and pleasure. More importantly, his use of magic to hide the rocks he cannot in fact destroy—rocks which stand for the evil that God inexplicably allows to exist in his world, as Dorigen's anguished speech makes clear (865–93)—parallels earlier attempts by Dorigen's friends to take her grieving mind off her absent husband by bringing her into the artful garden or attempting to include her in the dance (895–924). In all these cases, art cannot destroy evil or grief; art can only disguise them or divert attention from them. The ultimate practitioner of such a powerful but severely limited art is the Franklin himself, who manipulates his plot and characters so that all will turn out for the best—the situation is reversed at the last moment by no less than three consecutive acts of exemplary unselfishness by husband, would-be lover, and cleric-magician. Despite such "fredom" and "gentilesse" on all fronts, the black rocks remain at the end as they were at the beginning of the tale, an image of recalcitrant experience with its potential for calamity that art can hide but not, alas, destroy.

Perhaps the most interesting comment about art's ability to transform experience is supplied by the *Canon's Yeoman's Tale*.

[10]In Chaucer's immediate source, a story told by a character in Boccaccio's romance *Il Filocolo,* the magician is charged to—and does—make a real garden grow in January; the suitor brings fruit from it to the lady as proof. Chaucer's change establishes the limits of the magic. See further the unpublished dissertation of Joyce F. Leana, *Chaucer the Word-Master* (New York: Columbia University, 1973), to which I am much indebted with respect to the tales of the Franklin and the Canon's Yeoman.

With the late arrival of the Canon and his Yeoman among the
other pilgrims, Chaucer introduces a new kind of disruption of
order, this one from outside the "felaweship"; in so doing, he
also portrays a new aspect of experience: that of sheer physical
effort and exhaustion:

> His hakeney, that was al pomely grys,
> So swatte that it wonder was to see;
> ....
> The hors eek that his yeman rood upon
> So swatte that unnethe myghte it gon.
> Aboute the peytrel stood the foom ful hye;
> ....
> [The canon] hadde ay priked lik as he were wood
> ....
> But it was joye for to seen hym swete!
> His forheed dropped as a stillatorie,
> Were ful of plantayne and of paritorie.   (*CY Prol*, 569–81)

Here is poetry expressing the joy of sweat—but also, as the simile
of the "stillatorie" announces, a poetry entranced by technology.
Both these innovative interests loom large in the tale that follows,
as the Canon's Yeoman tells of the alchemist's attempt to turn
base metal into gold—a quest for the transformation of material
reality that can never succeed yet never be abandoned by its
obsessed practitioners (*CYT,* 862–83). The fruits of the quest are
not riches and power but exhaustion, debilitation, and endless
frustration lived out amidst the jargon and detritus of a world
brilliantly captured by Chaucer in literature's first depiction of
the laboratory of the mad scientist:

> Oure orpyment and sublymed mercurie,
> Oure grounden litarge eek on the porfurie,
> Of ech of thise of ounces a certayn—
> ....
> Oure urynales and oure descensories,
> Violes, crosletz, and sublymatories,
> Cucurbites and alambikes eek.
> ....
> Oure fourneys eek of calcinacioun,
> And of watres albificacioun;
> Unslekked lym, chalk, and gleyre of an ey,
> Poudres diverse asshes, donge, pisse and cley,   (774–807)

Existence in this nightmare world involves merciless exertion ("I blowe the fir til that myn herte feynte," 753), and the transformation wrought is not on metals but on people: wherever alchemists go, the Yeoman says, people know them by their smell of brimstone, threadbare clothes, and colorless visage (884–91; 1094–1100). Alchemists, in short, have their attempts to metamorphose reality rebound horribly on themselves, to the point where they become more devilish than human. (The Yeoman constantly compares the canon of his tale to the devil: "he was feendly both in werk and thoght," 1303.) Chaucer's tale is a devastating moral commentary on greed, illusion, and fraud—but it is also an audacious comparison of alchemy and his own art. For if alchemists degrade themselves into examples of the rubble amidst which they work, Chaucer the poet transforms the rubble, the "poudres diverse, asshes, donge, pisse and cley," of pseudoscience into art that is both didactic and pleasurable. Thanks to crooked alchemists, "al thyng which that shineth as the gold/ Nis nat gold" (962–63); given inspired poetry, human failure and technological jargon become both fascinating and beautiful. The *Canon's Yeoman's Tale* is a piece of self-congratulatory, bravura writing that forces us to acquiesce in the poet's self-conscious assessment of its effect: "but it *was* joye for to seen hym swete!"

Never one to rest on his laurels (or let his audience rest in its understanding), Chaucer offers as his last versified word in the *Canterbury Tales* the Manciple's story of a crow who could "countrefete the speche of every man . . . when he sholde telle a tale," (*ManT,* 134–35) and who is severely punished for telling an unpleasant truth. Since the Chaucerian narrator prefaces his own act of universal mimicry (including some quite unpleasant truths) with an earnest apology in the *General Prologue,* the effect of this last comic statement of the dangers of mimetic art is to bracket the entire, infinitely varied world of the *Canterbury Tales* within self-conscious acknowledgments that the closer art moves to experience, the more hazardous an undertaking it becomes. Presumably for Chaucer—and certainly for us—the pleasure of the game justifies the risks.

Emerson Brown, Jr.

Chaucer and the European Literary Tradition

> *For out of olde feldes, as men seyth,*
> *Cometh al this newe corn from yer to yere,*
> *And out of olde bokes, in good feyth,*
> *Cometh al this newe science that men lere.*
> —*Parliament of Fowls, 22–25*

Throughout his literary career, Chaucer borrowed plots, characters, settings, descriptive details, philosophical commentary, and verse forms from "olde bokes." Sometimes he translated other works virtually word for word. Sometimes he so transformed his sources that his own works resemble only slightly the texts on which they were based. Usually his poems are not simply translations, but they are close enough to known texts to appear to be adaptations rather than original compositions as we understand the term. Yet much great art is traditional rather than radically innovative. Homer, Sophocles, Virgil, and Shakespeare also depended on existing traditions. Further, according to the understanding of the creative process in the Middle Ages, the faculty that produces poetry is not imagination, as we might suppose, but memory. And it is, in part, the memory of old texts that provides the materials for new creations and new learning: "al this newe science that men lere."

The modern reader needs to know about the "olde bokes" from which Chaucer adapted material for his own poems. As we shall see, Chaucer depended on such knowledge on the part of his audience for certain kinds of meaning. Also, by following

Chaucer as he translates or reworks an earlier work, we can understand his intentions better as we see what he retains, what he eliminates, what he alters, emphasizes, or adds. Finally, although Chaucer is an innovative poet, he surely saw his poems not as radically new creations, breaking sharply with the past, but as works that derive part of their meaning from their position as the latest stage in a long, rich tradition. Thus the study of Chaucer and the European literary tradition involves not only "background information" but insights into Chaucer's poems themselves. We might begin by asking how this fourteenth-century Englishman learned to read foreign languages so well and what that ability did for him as a poet writing in English.

I

Chaucer probably began to learn foreign languages almost as soon as he began to learn English. As a child at home he would have received elementary instruction in reading and writing English and perhaps in French as well. Later, he almost certainly went to school. The Almonry School of St. Paul's Cathedral was near his home in London. Records of some of the books at St. Paul's show the wide range of readings in Latin which would have been available to young Geoffrey, and his own poetry reveals his familiarity with several of them. At such a school he would have been drilled on a few basic texts. Such intense study, often by rote memorization, continued well beyond the Middle Ages. We know of a sixteenth-century schoolboy who knew the elementary Latin grammar of Donatus by heart years before he learned to read and write! Chaucer may have been required to speak Latin rather than English or French to his teachers and fellow students.

Aside from formal schooling, however, and perhaps just as important as such study, Chaucer's day-to-day environment as he grew up in London provided him with great opportunities to hear and speak languages other than English. Chaucer's father was a prosperous vintner. The Chaucer family home was near the docks where ships came to unload wine from France or Spain. Though small by our standards, fourteenth-century London was a bustling, cosmopolitan city in which many foreigners lived. Chaucer grew up with French, Spanish, Italian, Flemish, and the many dialects of English ringing in his ears. It is no surprise, therefore, that he learned several foreign languages and learned them well. It may have been this proficiency gained rather early in life that made him valuable to have along on the many diplomatic missions of his later years. Chaucer was probably familiar with a great many languages, but three stand out as central in his literary career: Latin, French, and Italian.

From the moment of his baptism to his last conscious hours before death, Chaucer could hardly have gone through a day without experiencing Latin in some form. Latin was the universal language of medieval Europe. Acquiring Latin was the first task of every schoolboy, and advanced studies depended on it. Latin was the language of church services, of theology, of canon law, and of all the elaborate written communication needed to keep such a complex institution as the medieval church working smoothly. Latin was also the language of instruction in the universities, the language of scientific and philosophical thought, and a living literary language as well. Only educated people knew Latin, to be sure, and only a small percentage of the population was educated. But most educated people, by definition, knew some Latin, and this knowledge permitted easy communication among people of different countries and different languages. With the universal language came shared beliefs and ideas. There was a universal church in which virtually identical services were performed all over the Western world. The basic school curriculum, science, the Latin classics, philosophy, theology, mathematics, music, and law were all part of a shared intellectual heritage. And common traditions in such things as beast lore, astronomy, number symbolism, and the properties of precious stones brought people of different areas and different languages into the same community of ideas. Allusions to these traditions appear frequently in late medieval literature, sometimes in such subtle and indirect ways that the modern reader may not even realize what is happening. Serious students of Chaucer, therefore, need to learn something about this great heritage of the Latin learned tradition.

Although Chaucer knew none of the great Greek poets even in translation, he knew enough Latin to read the Latin classics, and there is strong evidence that he knew some of the classical writers very well. Precisely how good Chaucer was as a Latinist and which Latin texts he knew in the original are matters of continuing scholarly investigation. There is general agreement that Chaucer knew the *Liber Catonianus,* an anthology of Latin readings widely used in the schools. He knew Virgil and Statius, but Ovid stands out as his favorite Latin poet. Chaucer borrowed and alluded to stories and incidents from Ovid throughout his literary career. Richard L. Hoffman believes that "Chaucer considered Ovid an ethical philosopher and not merely a teller of tales" and that Chaucer "seems to have enjoyed representing himself as an English Ovid."

What does all this mean to us as readers of Chaucer? For one thing, it is important to remember that the great Latin writers had been rather thoroughly "medievalized." There was no doubt that they were pagans, living and dying outside of the Christian religion. Nevertheless, to many medieval thinkers their writings were inspired by God and contained Christian truths. In Dante's *Purgatory,* Statius credits Virgil with having shown him the way both to poetry and to Christianity: "Per te poeta fui, per te cristiano" (22.73). By means of elaborate commentaries, classical works were virtually re-created in medieval Christian terms. Thus, even at his most sensual and obscene, Ovid could be read as a moral poet. Further, the most popular classical texts and stories were more familiar to Chaucer and some members of his audience than they would be to all but a handful of classics majors today. Some of them, such as Claudius's *Rape of Proserpina* and Statius's *Achilleid* were read and reread in school. For some there were translations or retellings in vernacular languages. The *Ovide Moralisé,* for example, is a French verse translation of the *Metamorphoses* in which each story is followed by an elaborate Christian allegorization. Virgil's *Aeneid* had been retold in the Old French *Eneas.* The Thebes story was treated most thoroughly in Latin in the *Thebaid* of Statius and was also available to Chaucer in the Old French *Roman de Thèbes.* At the beginning of the second book of *Troilus and Criseyde,* Pandarus goes to visit his niece and finds her and two other ladies listening to a maiden read, somewhat anachronistically, a romance describing the seige of Thebes. The easy familiarity with the world of classical story which Chaucer weaves into the female society of Troy reflects the situation in his own sophisticated literary community.

Eventually, as the many contributors to the Chaucer library complete their work, we shall have new editions and English translations of all of the important Latin texts known to Chaucer. In the meantime, we need to bear in mind that apparently learned allusions to such texts may not have been nearly so forbidding to Chaucer's audience as they are to us. R. A. Pratt has shown, for example, that virtually all of the quotations from Seneca that Chaucer uses come not directly from the original texts but from popular handbooks assembled to give preachers a bit of learning the more to impress their flocks. By putting overworked moral sentiments from the revered "auctours" into the mouths of pompous and hypocritical speakers, Chaucer could comment on their learning and sincerity. Scholars show us the sources of Chaucer's classical learning, but ultimately we must decide for ourselves the intended effect of such learning. Rarely has a poet had so much confidence as Chaucer in the capacity of his audience to participate imaginatively in the creative relationship between text and reader that produces, in its fullest sense, the work of literature.

More than any English writer before his time and more than most who have followed, Chaucer absorbed the classical world as it was available to him and put it to complex poetic use as an accessible, natural part of his own creations. Sometimes Chaucer worked with the original Latin texts, sometimes from handbooks of excerpts or from translations, but, whatever his sources, he enriched his poems with classical material from the Ceyx and Alcione episode in the early *Book of the Duchess,* to the many classical allusions in *Troilus and Criseyde,* and to the dazzling array of allusion and episode in the *Merchant's Tale*. Chaucer's greatest models for the sophisticated use of classical materials were Dante, Petrarch, and Boccaccio. He may not rival their learning, but there is a wise and easy irreverence in Chaucer's use of classical setting, story, and allusion that betokens a humanism that is only different, not weaker, than that of his great Italian contemporaries. We are only beginning to understand the full effect of Chaucer's use of his classical literary backgrounds.

French was the foreign language Chaucer knew best. Although English was replacing it as the language of affairs in England during Chaucer's lifetime, French was still of great importance. Chaucer was nearly twenty before English was adopted as the language of the law courts or was first used for the opening speech of Parliament. The first English wills did not turn up for another twenty years, and even in 1386 Chaucer's deposition in the Scropes-Grosvenor controversy was taken in French. As a young man Chaucer served in aristocratic households where French was spoken and was sometimes the preferred language. The English aristocracy had been preoccupied with France for

300 years. This would continue well into the fifteenth century. English kings—themselves French in speech and descent—strove to control and expand their French landholdings. King Richard II, often called "Richard of Bordeaux" after the place of his birth, was quite French in his tastes. His second wife, Isabella, was the daughter of the French king. Chaucer's wife Phillippa was also French-speaking.

Although it is sometimes difficult to know for certain whether a given group of people in Chaucer's time spoke English or French in their daily lives, the prestige of French as a literary language is beyond question. Chaucer's contemporary, John Gower, wrote in French as well as in Latin and English. From the evidence of a list of books owned by King Richard in 1384 to 1385, his tastes were clearly for French literature, and the French poet and chronicler Jean Froissart presented him with a volume of his poems. The French knight and poet Oton de Graunson served the English king in war and lived for some time in England. Although we have no evidence that Chaucer himself wrote in French, he used French poetic forms, and his earliest known poems are either direct translations of French works (the *Romaunt of the Rose; An ABC*) or close imitations (several short lyrics, the *Book of the Duchess*). Chaucer turned to French translations when working with Latin and Italian texts, and French influences, far from being restricted to a single "French period" early in his poetic career, are found throughout his work. Chaucer knew personally several of the great French poets of his time. Eustache Deschamps addressed to him a ballade, the refrain of which indicates how closely Chaucer's contemporary reputation was allied with his transmission of French materials: "Grant translateur, noble Geffroy Chaucier."

The single French poem of greatest influence in fourteenth-century France and England was *Le Roman de la Rose*. Guillaume de Lorris began the poem in the 1230s. Some forty years later, Jean de Meun wrote a vast continuation that brought the complete poem to nearly 22,000 verses. The *Roman* is a dream vision poem. It is stylized and courtly in Guillaume's part, more learned and intellectually challenging in Jean's. The relationship between the two parts and among the many episodes and digressions within Jean's part are controversial matters that cannot detain us here. The important point is that Chaucer himself translated the *Roman* and that it influenced his poetry throughout his life. It is a poem that serious readers of Chaucer ought to know, and two recent English translations make it easy to do so. In fourteenth-century France, dream vision poems, particularly as vehicles for exploring different aspects of love, continued to be very popular. Chaucer wrote three dream visions, the first of which, the *Book of the Duchess,* shows how early in his career Chaucer learned to combine elaborate borrowings from previous literature with great originality. The *Book of the Duchess* is a patchwork quilt of quotations from French poets, especially from Guillaume de Machaut, and yet it is at the same time an independent work, different from the tradition it relies on for so many of its particular details.

As we reflect on the immense debt English literature owes to French influence, it is sad to recall that during centuries of fruitful intellectual communication the two peoples have often been opposed in bitter, savage warfare. Chaucer the young squire was captured while on a military expedition near the city of Rheims, which the English had under seige. Ironically, at that time Guillaume de Machaut, to whom Chaucer the writer was to owe so much, was canon of the city. But while the French and English armies have clashed, there have always been Frenchmen and Englishmen who have felt themselves to be united by a common cultural heritage. Geoffrey Chaucer may have been such a person. Of French name and most likely of French ancestry, he was an acquaintance and translator of French poets, a diplomat to France, husband of a French-speaking wife, and a poet to a court with French tastes. To my French acquaintances I have jokingly referred to "Geffroy Chaucier" as the greatest French poet of the Middle Ages—except for the fact that he wrote in English! That is not quite true, of course, for Chaucer is an English poet in more than the language of his verse. But while we can imagine him becoming a very good poet without ever setting foot in Italy or reading a word of Italian, we can hardly imagine him becoming a poet at all without the incalculable influence of France.

Yet important as French influence was, the greatest literature of fourteenth-century Europe came not from France but from Italy—from the Florence of Dante, Petrarch, and Boccaccio. Chaucer's obvious debts to these writers have long been recognized. The reader who knows little else about Chaucer's sources knows that the *Troilus* is based on Boccaccio's *Filostrato* and that the *Knight's Tale* is based on his *Teseida.* Chaucer's direct debts to Dante and Petrarch are less extensive, but they have also been well documented. What needs further study is the more subtle influence of the Italians. How did Chaucer's familiarity with Dante, Petrarch, and Boccaccio help him to see, to understand, and to write more effectively than he might have without them? In what subtle ways not detectable in verbal echoes did they influence his attitudes toward love, toward nobility, toward the moral responsibility of the artist? In attempting to answer such questions we may find that Dante, rather than Boccaccio, will prove to have had the greatest impact on Chaucer. In the *Commedia* Dante combined absolutely precise and realistic particularity of character, setting, and incident with profound universal significance. The *Commedia* is clearly allegorical, clearly exemplary fiction, and yet it reads like history. We see it, and, giving ourselves over to it, we believe it happened. Perhaps no poem in all of world literature achieves a more perfect fusion of realistic surface narrative and multivalent significance. Now Dante did not invent such a fusion of realism and allegory. We find the same sort of thing everywhere in medieval literature, quite prominently, for example, in the *Roman de la Rose*. But Dante perfected it.

Chaucer mined the works of Boccaccio for some of his greatest stories, but he may have reached back past Boccaccio to Dante for the capacity to present characters both as collections of attributes signaling various moral abstractions and as irreducible, individual human beings, moving about in a real world at a specific historical moment. The Wife of Bath is a more satisfactory character than La Vieille not only because she is more "realistic" but also because she *means* more. That advance from the *Roman de la Rose* to the *Canterbury Tales* may be attributable at least in part to Chaucer's study of Dante. Be that as it may, Dante also plays a more tangible role in Chaucer's development as a poet.

Chaucer wrote the *House of Fame* with Dante's *Commedia* very much in mind. Whether the role of the *Commedia* is central or peripheral, all agree that the *House of Fame* contains many elements from it and that Chaucer's attitude toward that great poem in the *House of Fame* is not one of solemn reverence. Fame herself, as she blithely and capriciously metes out fame and ignominy, may be a parody of Dante. The unsympathetic reader of the *Commedia* might accuse Dante of doing the same thing as he assigns his Florentine friends and enemies to their niches in Hell, Purgatory, and Heaven. What can a poet do who finds himself living in the shadow of an acknowledged masterpiece that he fears he is incapable of equaling? One thing he can do is turn to parody. Some parodies, like the mock epic *Rape of the Lock,* written in the shadow of *Paradise Lost,* assume a greatness as independent works. The *House of Fame,* however, does not achieve that independent stature. Incomplete and uneven, it is delightful to read but frustrating to understand. Perhaps it is best seen as a kind of exercise, an early and ultimately unsatisfactory attempt to deal with the challenge presented by Dante's *Commedia.* Many years went by before Chaucer returned again to that challenge. When he did return, it was not to parody Dante but—in his own way—to surpass him. He returned in the *Canterbury Tales.*

Dante's *Commedia* is a pilgrimage, and Dante is the pilgrim. It is another version of the *Itinerarium mentis ad deum*—the journey of the mind to God—given a life and depth that no mystical journey had ever been given before. That is one structure, of literature and of life. Man is thought of as a traveler, *homo viator* in the medieval phrase, and in the *Commedia* the whole meaning of life is depicted as finding the proper way to make one's journey to heaven. The pleasures of this world can be used but only as necessary pauses in one's journey, not as ends in themselves. So it is that in the second Canto of *Purgatory* when Dante and the spirits pause to listen to a love song, stern old Cato stirs them into movement, berating them for their laziness (2.118–23).

There is, however, another view of life and of literature, a view that insists that the pleasures of this world may be enjoyed not simply to refresh us and to aid us in our journey but as ends in themselves. So at Florence in plague time, ten attractive young people leave the horrors of the city to wander idly through the idealized landscape of Boccaccio's *Decameron.* They tell their stories, moving from wild and magnificent obscenity to a kind of peace as the last tale leads them to contemplate the virtuous patience of Griselda. Then they return to Florence. That is another kind of structure. Old Cato certainly would not approve of pausing for fifteen days to enjoy the delights of pastoral life and storytelling, but Boccaccio seems to. Chaucer may not have known the *Decameron,* though he could have. But the view of life it depicts was available to him through the Goliards, through Horace, and through, one is tempted to add, life itself. It was also available by negative example through the whole *homo viator* tradition, through Dido's distraction of Aeneas, through the morbid message of the *ubi sunt* lyric tradition, and, of course, through Dante.

In the *Canterbury Tales* Chaucer harmonizes, consciously or unconsciously, the basic philosophies of those two very different Italian works. Like the *Commedia,* the *Canterbury Tales* is a pilgrimage. We are constantly reminded of our journey, however stumbling it may be, towards the holy place. But like the *Decameron,* the *Canterbury Tales* depicts a world where earthly values and the literatures of entertainment have a place. Such values are finally superseded as the pilgrims gather for their last tale close to the holy shrine, but Chaucer has taken all of them and all of the stories they tell that far. If we are ever tempted to doubt the breadth and depth of Chaucer's humanity, we need only picture Dante taking the Miller, the Merchant, Alison of Bath, and their tales along with him on his journey to the stars. Dante, the greater poet if not the warmer soul, made his pilgrimage without those useless but invaluable pauses which certain kinds of art require, and he made his pilgrimage alone.

II

After such generalizations concerning the influence of Latin, French, and Italian literature on Chaucer's work, it might be useful to examine some specific instances in which familiarity with the traditions behind Chaucer's poetry enables us to read it more intelligently.

The *General Prologue* to the *Canterbury Tales* used to be treated as an example of how Chaucer's native English talent blossomed as his careful observation of "life itself" replaced his earlier dependence on French and Italian sources. Yet scholarly investigation has shown again and again that the portraits in the *General Prologue,* far from being drawn simply "from life," are packed with details that send the reader to learned traditions for their meaning. Just recently we have learned that the whole *General Prologue* becomes more meaningful when seen in its proper literary context.

Sources and Analogues (see the Bibliographic Note at the end of this article) begins with a chapter on the "Literary Framework of the *Canterbury Tales*." Yet that very good chapter overlooks the basic literary genre of the *Prologue*. Jill Mann shows the close connection of the *General Prologue* with the widespread medieval tradition of satire based on the failings of the different social classes. By seeing the *General Prologue* against the background of dozens of works (chiefly in Latin and French) in the tradition of estates satire, we have a far clearer idea of what Chaucer's governing principles and his own particular contributions are. Once again we see how understanding increases with awareness of Chaucer's position within the European literary tradition.

Turning from Chaucer's use of a large organizing principle like estates satire to his adaptation of shorter passages within larger works, we might recall how often the notes in scholarly editions of Chaucer indicate that a given line or group of lines comes from some earlier work. The *Merchant's Tale* has been called a "dense mosaic of allusions, references, and quotations," and the same might be said of many of Chaucer's poems. How are we as readers to react to such a technique? Since many of the passages Chaucer adapts from other works were already familiar to his audience in their original context, Chaucer's use of them involves much more than lazy or unimaginative "borrowing." He would expect the more learned and perceptive members of his audience to recognize that a character, descriptive passage, or piece of moralizing came from a specific context, and he would expect them to be capable of bringing that context to bear in interpreting the passage as it functions in the new work. Some examples may make this very common technique clear.

It has long been known that Chaucer borrows many details from the *Roman de la Rose* in his description of the Prioress's table manners:

> At mete wel ytaught was she with alle:
> She leet no morsel from hir lippes falle,
> Ne wette hir fyngres in hir sauce depe;
> Wel koude she carie a morsel and wel kepe
> That no drope ne fille upon hire brest.
> In curteisie was set ful muchel hir lest.
> Hir over-lippe wyped she so clene
> That in hir coppe ther was no ferthyng sene
> Of grece, when she dronken hadde hir draughte.
> Ful semely after hir mete she raughte.   (*Gen Prol,* 127–36)

The relevant lines from the *Roman* are as follows:

Let her guard against getting her fingers wet up to the joint in the sauce, against smearing her lips with soup, garlic, or fat meat, against piling up too large morsels and stuffing her mouth. When she has to moisten a piece of sauce, either *sauce verte, cameline,* or *jauce,* she should hold the bit with her fingertips and bring it carefully up to her mouth, so that no drop of soup, sauce, or pepper falls on her breast. She must drink so neatly that she doesn't spill anything on herself, for anyone who happened to see her spill would think her either very clumsy or very greedy. Again, she must take care not to touch her drinking cup while she has food in her mouth. She should wipe her mouth so clean that grease will not stick to the cup, and should be particularly careful about her upper lip, for, when there is grease on it, untidy drops of it will show in her wine. (Dahlberg translation, p. 231)

The *Roman* was one of the most popular poems in the Middle Ages. Chaucer himself translated it into English. He could not have expected his audience to overlook the source of the passage describing the Prioress's etiquette. To the contrary, his meaning depends in part on having the audience recognize the passage, recall its context in the *Roman,* and associate the affected gentility of the Prioress with the instructions a wordly wise old woman gives to a young girl to teach her to be attractive to men. The Prioress acts as though she were applying the lessons of La Vieille to her own life, and those are hardly the sort of lessons a prioress should be heeding. This passage is not simply a borrowing from another literary work but an allusion to it. All of Chaucer's borrowings may be, in effect, allusions. Chaucer leads us to think about the original context of a borrowed passage and to use our imaginations in interpreting his new use of that context. Earl Wasserman spells out this technique of reading certain kinds of poetry in his famous essay on the *Rape of the Lock*. What he says about Pope's allusions is equally applicable to Chaucer. If we are to concentrate on "the poem itself," we must broaden our definition of the poem to include passages and whole literary contexts which the poem alludes to.

While the description of the Prioress's table manners leads the perceptive reader to a single work of literature, at other times Chaucer alludes to more widely diffused traditions. R. E. Kaske has shown how Aleyn's farewell speech to Malyne in the *Reeve's Tale* parodies in the medieval dawn song:

> Aleyn was wery in the dawenynge,
> For he had swonken al the longe nyght,
> And seyde, "Fare weel, Malyne, sweete wight!
> The day is come, I may no lenger byde;
> But everemo, wher so I go or ryde,
> I is thyn awen clerk, swa have I seel!"   (4234–39)

Since the richest collection of extant medieval dawn songs is in German, a language Chaucer apparently did not know, and since few examples survive in the languages that he clearly did know, here the task of the scholar is more complicated than it is with allusions to a single known source. The benefits to the reader are no less valuable, however. Kaske shows the sort of romantic, "courtly" context in which the dawn songs occurred. Then by indicating how Chaucer violates the dawn song tradition to wildly comic effect, he transforms a passage that seems pointless and destructive of the fabliau mood into a richly meaningful piece of comedy. Far from leading us away from the text, Kaske's discussion of other poems in the dawn-song tradition makes us aware, for the first time, of what the text of those lines in the *Reeve's Tale* really is. Chaucer wrote them with a certain tradition in mind, and he expected his public to recall that tradition when they read (or heard) the lines. Until we become aware of that tradition, the lines as Chaucer intended them can scarcely be said to exist.

Similar, though on a larger scale, is the relationship of Chaucer's so-called fabliaux to the folktales and verse narratives from which they are directly or indirectly derived. These ancient tales were widely diffused in medieval Europe, and they must have been known to Chaucer's audience. With the basic plot a matter of common knowledge, the interest of the audience would not be in what happens but in how the story is told. Part of the excitement "opening night audiences" must have felt when Chaucer read one of his poems was the joy of recognizing, after hundreds of lines of imaginative introductory material, the emergence of some old, well-known story. Read one of the close analogues to the *Miller's Tale* or the *Merchant's Tale,* for example, and then notice how far into Chaucer's version you get before it becomes clear just what story you are reading. With the creation of characters of far greater complexity than those in the usual fabliau, with the addition of whole new episodes, with allusions to Ovid, and the Bible, and the whole vast learned tradition of medieval Europe, Chaucer builds layer upon layer of meaning on these tired old plots. The tales that emerge from this process are marvelous, simply in isolation, but, by then putting them into the dramatic context of the Canterbury pilgrimage, Chaucer adds further significance. Finally, I believe, that act of assigning these tales to specific narrators, and often to spectacularly imperfect if not downright limited ones, forces a moral evaluation of the literary forms themselves. What kind of person believes that plots turning on trickery, adultery, and the triumph of deception are worth telling? Why do certain people tell certain stories in certain ways? In the *Merchant's Tale,* for example, through the prologue to the tale and through numerous details within the tale itself, Chaucer makes us aware of a misogynistic, materialistic, cynical narrator, matched to the tale he tells. At the same time that we enjoy a tale like the Merchant's, we realize that the form of literature to which it belongs is being subtly evaluated.

What must have constantly dazzled Chaucer's audience was the magic of his genius as he transformed old stories into masterpieces of multivalent poetry. But to experience the originality of Chaucer's brilliant retellings of these old tales, we need to know them as his audience did. Until recently this was not easy, for many of the analogues to Chaucer's fabliaux had not been translated into English. Now, Larry D. Benson and Theodore Andersson have provided the original texts and English translations for many stories that show us the kind of material that Chaucer and his audience would have known. With their book in hand, the beginning reader of Chaucer's fabliaux can approach them with some of the knowledge that Chaucer might have assumed in his audience.

One could list almost endlessly examples of how the literary backgrounds of Chaucer's poems can be used to deepen our understanding. So far I have been assuming that Chaucer might have anticipated this knowledge in at least the more sophisticated members of his audience. There may be cases, however, where the audience may not have known what source or sources Chaucer was using. If Chaucer did not expect his audience to know a poem he was reworking, does it profit us to treat that poem as relevant to our efforts to understand Chaucer? This is not an easy matter to resolve, but finally I think we are justified in using all the resources we have to see how any poem came into being. For one thing, we simply cannot be sure of everything that Chaucer's audience did and did not know. They had to have known the plots of such tales as the Merchant's and the Miller's, but did they know the source of the *Troilus,* and did Chaucer therefore expect them to see through his attribution of that story to one "Lollius"? Or was he seriously attempting to conceal his source? Yet, however obscure a poet's sources may be, the poet could hardly expect every single member of his audience, present and future, to remain forever ignorant of them. The subtle, ironic poet knows that his audience is made up of many sorts of people who will respond to his poetry with many levels of comprehension. To return to the example of the Prioress, some will miss the irony entirely and will admire her fine manners. Others will recognize that there is something wrong with her but will not know the *Roman de la Rose* and will respond only vaguely to the signals Chaucer sets forth in his echoes of that poem. Some will know the *Roman* and will respond more fully. But the more we know, the closer we come to that fullest understanding that was Chaucer's own. That is the way the ironic writer works. He leads us to believe that there are some members of his audience who will never quite grasp his basic point, but that we are special—we know what he *really* means. We never reach that fullest understanding, of course, but as we read Chaucer and the many works from many languages by means of which he created his own literary world, we come closer and closer. I cannot believe that Chaucer would find that disconcerting.

As students of English literature, we are tempted to look back on Chaucer as the beginning, as the first great poet in the English language. But it is far closer to the truth to view Chaucer as standing at the end of a long literary tradition. We should think of him not as a single brilliant jewel sparkling in splendid isolation on a velvet cushion of "classical and European backgrounds" but rather as one particularly brilliant figure among many others in a tapestry crowded with the poets and thinkers of 1,500 years of the European literary tradition. The ideal reader of Chaucer would be able to move as easily among the languages and literatures of fourteenth-century London as Chaucer and the most learned members of his audience could. That may not be a reasonable goal for most of us. But aided by the painstaking and invaluable work of generations of medieval scholars, we can begin to approach that ideal. We can begin to see the figure of Chaucer in its full brilliance in that rich tapestry that was the multilingual, highly self-conscious and articulate intellectual world of late medieval Europe.

It was a world, however, that Chaucer may have sensed to be in its final days. So in time of plague, and war, and schism, social unrest and institutional breakdown, Chaucer gathered together the literary treasures from the past and, with the power of his genius, transformed them to last for a future he could scarcely have believed possible. In his last great work, Chaucer moved with the pilgrims of his imagination along the laughter-filled and winding road to Canterbury. It is a human pilgrimage with human pilgrims moving along a very real road. It is also a literary pilgrimage, as the genres, plots, characters, settings, shallow pomposity, and unfathomable wisdom of 1,500 years of European literature reveal their strengths and weaknesses in the lists of "sentence" and "solas." As Chaucer moves towards Canterbury, he takes up these forms, one by one, from romance to fabliau, saint's life to beast fable, Breton lay to tragedy, hypocritical sermon and pious homily. A world of genres mirrors a world of themes, tellers, and places: Thebes and Athens and Oxenford, Syria, St. Denis, Flanders, Pavia, and Rome. Through all these tales, all these genres, settings, and narrative styles, Chaucer evaluates the whole European literary tradition and his own uses of it as he sets its rich forms as stages along the way to Canterbury. By telling tales of Athens, Rome, and Trumpington, Chaucer leads us to the holy shrine. And at the end of that pilgrimage it is right that there should be no more tales to tell.

BIBLIOGRAPHICAL NOTE

An essay attempting to discuss such a vast topic as Chaucer's classical and continental literary backgrounds must depend heavily on the work of others. The information contained here comes from such a wide variety of reading over the years that it would be difficult to attribute it to its proper sources even if I had chosen to burden the reader with the sort of footnotes that such attribution would require. What follows is a list of some of the most important books and articles I have consulted and of all the books and articles I have specifically referred to. Hopefully it will serve both as some indication of my many debts and as a list of useful further reading for those who wish to delve deeper into the subject.

All known records pertaining to Chaucer's life are brought together in the *Chaucer Life-Records,* Martin M. Crow and Clair C. Olson, eds. (Austin: University of Texas Press, 1966).

Perhaps the best general introduction to childhood and early education in medieval Europe is Philippe Ariès, *Centuries of Childhood: A Social History of Family Life,* Robert Baldick, trans. (New York: Vintage Books, 1962). Useful for many aspects of Chaucer's environment is *Chaucer's World,* a collection of original medieval documents compiled by Edith Rickert and edited by Clair C. Olson and Martin M. Crow (New York: Columbia University Press, 1948; paperback ed. 1962): documents pertaining to medieval education are on pp. 101–36. Concerning Richard II's tastes in literature, see Edith Rickert, "King Richard II's Books," *Library,* ser. 4, 13 (1932), 144–47.

A readable introduction to the bookish heritage of the Latin learned tradition is C. S. Lewis, *The Discarded Image* (Cambridge: at the University Press, 1964; paperback ed. 1967). All serious readers of medieval literature should be familiar with Ernst Robert Curtius, *European Literature and the Latin Middle Ages,* Willard R. Trask, trans. (New York: Harper Torchbooks ed., 1963). A useful short introduction is Robert W. Ackerman, *Backgrounds to Medieval English Literature* (New York: Random House, 1966). The most accessible source of information about the particular details behind individual passages in Chaucer's poetry is still the explanatory notes in Robinson's second edition of the complete *Works.*

For Chaucer's use of the Latin classics, a very good short introduction with a good bibliography is Richard L. Hoffman, "The Influence of the Classics on Chaucer," in the *Companion to Chaucer Studies,* Beryl Rowland, ed. (Toronto: Oxford University Press, 1968), pp. 162–75. The quotations from Hoffman are from that article. R. A. Pratt has several useful articles concerning the sources of Chaucer's classical learning; note especially "Chaucer and the Hand that Fed Him," *Speculum,* 41 (1966), 619–42.

Also in the *Companion to Chaucer Studies* is Haldeen Braddy, "The French Influence on Chaucer," pp. 123–38. The standard treatment is Charles Muscatine, *Chaucer and the French Tradition: A Study in Style and Meaning* (Berkeley: University of California Press, 1964). The *Romance of the Rose* is now available in a modern English verse translation by Harry W. Robbins (New York: E. P. Dutton, 1962) and in a prose translation by Charles Dahlberg (Princeton, N.J.: Princeton University Press, 1971). Concerning the French backgrounds of the *Book of the Duchess,* see James I. Wimsatt, *Chaucer and the French Love Poets: The Literary Background of the* Book of the

Duchess (Chapel Hill: University of North Carolina Press, 1968). Valuable for students of Chaucer is William Calin, *A Poet at the Fountain: Essays on the Narrative Verse of Guillaume de Machaut* (Lexington, Ky.: The University Press of Kentucky, 1974).

A good introduction to Chaucer's Italian backgrounds is Paul G. Ruggiers, "The Italian Influence on Chaucer," in the *Companion to Chaucer Studies,* pp. 139–61. Boccaccio's *Teseida* has recently been translated into English by Bernadette Marie McCoy as *The Book of Theseus* (New York: Teesdale Publishing Associates, 1974). For its importance to Chaucer see R. A. Pratt, "Chaucer's Use of the *Teseida,*" *Publications of the Modern Language Association,* 62 (1947), 598–621.

For the theme of man as the traveler, see Gerhart B. Ladner, *"Homo Viator:* Mediaeval Ideas on Alienation and Order," *Speculum,* 42 (1967), 233–59.

Of great value in understanding the significance of many allusions to medieval science is Walter Clyde Curry, *Chaucer and the Mediaeval Sciences,* 2nd ed. (New York: Barnes and Noble, 1960). The literary backgrounds of the *Canterbury Tales* are collected and discussed in *Sources and Analogues of Chaucer's* Canterbury Tales, W. F. Bryan and Germaine Dempster, eds. (Chicago, University of Chicago Press: 1941; reprinted New York: Humanities Press, 1958). Essential for understanding the genre of the *General Prologue* is Jill Mann, *Chaucer and Medieval Estates Satire* (Cambridge University Press, 1973).

Concerning the technique of reading complex literary allusion, see Earl Wasserman, "The Limits of Allusion in *The Rape of the Lock,*" *Journal of English and Germanic Philology,* 65 (1966), 425–44; Richard Hazleton, "The *Manciple's Tale:* Parody and Critique," *Journal of English and Germanic Philology,* 62 (1963); and R. E. Kaske, "Patristic Exegesis in the Criticism of Medieval Literature: The Defense," in *Critical Approaches to Medieval Literature: Selected Papers from the English Institute,* 1958–59, Dorothy Bethurum, ed. (New York; Columbia University Press, 1960), pp. 27–60. For the dawn-song tradition and the *Reeve's Tale* see R. E. Kaske, "An Aube in the *Reeve's Tale,*" *ELH, A Journal of English Literary History,* 26 (1959), 295–310. Useful for understanding Chaucer's fabliaux is Larry D. Benson and Theodore M. Andersson, *The Literary Context of Chaucer's Fabliaux: Texts and Translations* (Indianapolis and New York: Bobbs-Merrill, 1971).

Esther C. Quinn

Religion in Chaucer's Canterbury Tales:
A Study in Language and Structure*

The enormous and controversial subject of religion in the poetry of Chaucer might best be approached in a brief study by beginning with two generally accepted points: Chaucer was living in an age dominated by religious forces, and his poetry is permeated with religious references. Although the pervasive influence of religion on the poetry of Chaucer is widely recognized in numerous articles, notes in standard editions, and comments in book-length studies, there is no single comprehensive study of the subject. Views range from the representation of Chaucer as the mouthpiece for the religious didacticism of the age to Chaucer as an amiable, forward-looking hedonist who rejected religion as superstition. In our effort to arrive at a fair assessment, we should concede that Chaucer does not seem to be primarily a religious poet, like Dante and Langland. Indeed, we have a kind of paradox that calls for exploration: a poet living in a predominantly religious milieu, writing poetry permeated with religious references, who nevertheless is often bawdy and satirical and who impresses many readers as worldly, skeptical, or even cynical.

We shall approach the matter first by singling out from the complex world of fourteenth-century religion some of the elements that especially interested Chaucer; second by considering the relationship between religious language, which occurs throughout Chaucer's work, and religious structure, a somewhat more elusive concept; and finally by analyzing the way some of

*This essay is taken from a book-length study I am preparing on religious elements in Chaucer's poetry; it is part excerpt and part summary.

the religious elements appear as language and as structure in several of the *Canterbury Tales,* for it is on the pilgrimage to Canterbury that we can best trace the impact of fourteenth-century religion on Chaucer's poetry.

To a considerable extent, the religious language in Chaucer is a reflection of the dominating influence of the culture, which was, in externals at least, Christian. The frequency with which Chaucer's contemporaries referred to Christ, Mary, and the saints is echoed in his poetry, in the language of the pilgrims and in the tales they tell, especially those set in the Christian Era. But Chaucer is an artist and does not merely echo conventional pieties (or impieties); rather, as we shall see, he uses religious language in a variety of contexts, and it is only by considering the language in relation to the structure that we can arrive at his meaning.

Since religion played a significant role both in the real world of fourteenth-century England and in the world of Chaucer's poetry, we should consider first some of the aspects of the religion of his time that interested Chaucer and then explore, through an analysis of the religious language and structure, the way in which he transformed these real but transient aspects of the religion of his day into something fictitious but permanent.

Of the varied and complex world of fourteenth-century Christianity, certain aspects particularly interested Chaucer. A rough indication of his interests can be gauged by considering specific references, though ultimately the more accurate indication of his religious interests will be found in imaginative constructs rather than in the explicit use of religious language. A number of religious terms appear in a variety of contexts, which we might call key religious words. They not only recur throughout the text of the *Canterbury Tales* but also figure as structural units.

One of the most important of these key religious words, and the best one to begin with, is "pilgrimage." Pilgrimages were only one of the many aspects of fourteenth-century religious life to which Chaucer responded as a poet, but the fact that he made his *Canterbury Tales* one great pilgrimage suggests that the custom of pilgrimage became for him the concept of pilgrimage. In it are included all the elements of religion that interested him.

A pilgrimage was originally a spontaneous act of religious devotion, a journey to a distant holy site, a perilous undertaking involving hardship and sacrifice. The Christian practice of pilgrimage began in the early centuries following the death of Jesus and represented the desire of the faithful to walk upon the land where the Savior walked and thereby draw closer to his holy presence. By the third century, Christian pilgrims were making their way to the Holy Land. Over the centuries, the custom of making pilgrimages spread and pilgrimage sites multiplied, extending outward from Jerusalem and Bethlehem to Rome, Compostella, Cologne, and Bologna. By the fourteenth century, Canterbury had become England's most popular pilgrimage site, and Saint Thomas of Becket, England's greatest martyr-saint.

A great deal separates the sacrificial death of Jesus on Calvary and the murder of the archbishop in his cathedral at Canterbury. But they had this in common: the belief that a martyrdom had occurred, that the site of this martyrdom was sacred, and that to visit the site was to derive some of the material and spiritual benefits of the martyr's death.

What Chaucer knew or how he felt about the quarrel between Becket and his king which led to the archbishop's murder one can only speculate. But in the course of his *Canterbury Tales* Chaucer shows, besides his interest in the pilgrimage to Canterbury, a multitude of references to saints, martyrs, miracles, and relics.

By the fourteenth century, a pilgrimage for the most part was no longer an individual act of piety but rather a group undertaking in which religious motives play a part, yet the desire for companionship, pleasure, profit, or mere restlessness might figure more strongly. However great the contrast between the motley company that sets out from the Tabard Inn on that April morning and the archetypal act of devotion that led men to seek God at a particular site, the pilgrimage was still in Chaucer's day an essentially religious event, and reminders of this fact occur throughout the fictional pilgrimage.

The opening movement of the *Canterbury Tales,* with its lovely description of an April morning, suggests the beginning of the world, when all things were fresh and new. April is a time to celebrate; April is full of promise. But as the poem progresses, the ways of fallen humanity intrude: drunkenness, quarreling, and swearing among the pilgrims, and in the tales they tell—cheating, vengeance, and murder.

April may also be the Christian penitential season of Lent. Although in the beginning of the pilgrimage the sense of joyous

anticipation is strong and there are few indications of the penitential possibility, references to Lent and to penance do crop up, and
by the end the penitential aspect is sounded clearly. The words
"penance" and "penitence," used in a number of contexts as the
pilgrims make their way to Canterbury, serve as reminders of the
penitential possibility, and the theme of penitence appears
strongly at the end in the tale of the Parson, with his reminder that
people will be forgiven if they will truly repent. The fictional
pilgrimage rests upon the doctrines of the Fall and the Redemp-
tion; the structure of the *Canterbury Tales* parallels the Creation,
Fall, and the promise of restoration to grace. There are other
structures within the tales, but this is the structure of the pilgrimage.

By his use of the pilgrimage framework, Chaucer establishes
the religious point of view from which we are to evaluate the
characters, actions, and tales. Into the framework of a pilgrimage
Chaucer has drawn a wide variety of religious elements from the
Christian world of his own day. And the tale-telling scheme enables him, through fictional excursions into earlier times and distant places, to incorporate elements of paganism and primitive
Christianity.

The pilgrimage toward Canterbury, though grounded in the
reality of fourteenth-century English life by a multitude of
specific references, is a conceptual pilgrimage. Chaucer moves
from the actual custom of erring humans making pilgrimages into
the idea of pilgrimage. In the Parson the actual and conceptual
pilgrimages meet. To him the pilgrimage is an opportunity to join
his sinful fellow pilgrims, to listen to them, and to urge them to
repent. The pilgrimage is a metaphor for humanity's journey from
a physical toward a spiritual reality. Few would claim that
Chaucer's chief intent in writing the *Canterbury Tales* was either
to express religious devotion or to point out the need for reform,
but his choice of a pilgrimage as an organizing principle points to
his acceptance of a religious dimension of reality that could be
transformed into art. His use of the pilgrimage serves a number of
purposes: it is a reminder of a religious environment, of religious
values, and of a religious possibility.

The way Chaucer uses pilgrimage is typical of the way he
uses a number of religious elements: he takes, in this instance, a
religious custom and, by using the word in a number of contexts,
creates both a concept of pilgrimage and a structure of pilgrimage.
By examining the context in which actual references to pilgrimage

occur, we can trace the interaction between the word "pilgrimage" and the structure of a pilgrimage. As we shall discover, Chaucer uses the device of pilgrimage to balance the possibility of religious devotion against the actuality of humanity's fallen state. References to pilgrimages and pilgrims occur not only in connection with the journey to Canterbury but in the tales the pilgrims tell and, more importantly, in the remarks of the Parson at the end. More significant than the references to the actual pilgrimage or even the metaphorical uses of the word is the pilgrimage as structure: the pilgrims moving from inn toward cathedral, from the Host's storytelling game to the Parson's treatise on penitence.

Although the pilgrimage is essentially a religious custom, the motives of individual pilgrims range from religious to irreligious. The primarily religious motivations might include seeking cures or favors or giving thanks for cures or favors received, assuaging a sense of guilt, or completing a penance imposed by one's confessor.

Although a pilgrimage might be undertaken for penitential reasons, there is little sense of this in the beginning of Chaucer's Canterbury pilgrimage. As the pilgrims start out from the Tabard Inn with the innkeeper as their self-proclaimed guide, having agreed to participate in his tale-telling game, the religious, especially the penitential, aspect of pilgrimage is minimized. It is easy to lose one's sense of the pilgrimage as a religious event because many of the pilgrims are such rascals: they drink to excess, swear, quarrel, deceive others and themselves; in short, they exhibit every form of vice and folly. And yet the sinful state of a considerable number of this heterogeneous company should come as no surprise to anyone familiar with the doctrine of the Fall. Regardless of their behavior or motivation, they are Christians, fallen, in need of salvation. They are all members of a pilgrim community, united in being Canterbury-bound English Christians of the fourteenth century, the pilgrim-creations of Chaucer, brought into being by him to participate in his pilgrimage of pilgrimages.

The explicit purpose of the pilgrimage is religious, but the gathering of the pilgrims at the Tabard Inn, the physical point of departure, with all its associations of food, drink, lodging, and conviviality, establishes humanity's physical dimension. The pilgrims' easy acceptance of the innkeeper who proclaims himself their "governour" (*Gen Prol,* 813), and their ready assent to his proposal that they engage in a tale-telling competition with the promise of a supper as the reward, serve as reminders of humanity's susceptibility to being led and misled.

It is the Host who sets the holiday mood, whose strong physical presence establishes the spirit of festivity. This holiday spirit, however, is disrupted from time to time by quarrels. Both the festive mood and the religious intention are marred by quarreling, but paradoxically these quarrels both enliven the poem and, by exposing fraudulent pretensions, serve an essentially religious purpose. Several times in the course of the pilgrimage quarrels erupt and peace is restored. In this pattern of quarrels and reconciliations that is interwoven in the tale-telling, the Host plays a dual role: he alternately engages in quarrels and acts as peacemaker. It is he—"boold of his speche" (755)—who obscenely insults the Pardoner and exposes his aggressive fraudulence to derisive laughter. Here, ironically, it is the Knight, whose whole life has been spent in riding out on military expeditions, who intervenes as peacemaker. The Host not only insults the Pardoner, who richly deserves the insult, but he and the Shipman speak derisively of the good Parson. In the end, however, the Parson plays his true role: he refuses to tell a fable, or a tale in verse, or to use alliteration; he preaches a plain sermon on penitence. He finally prevails as the guide to the shrine of shrines in the Heavenly City. Chaucer's pilgrims represent a whole range of human possibility: they vary in temperament from quarrelsome to peace-loving, in behavior from models of Christian charity to unscrupulous rascals. But, however varied the company, regardless of motive or mode of life, they are all fourteenth-century English Christians riding toward the shrine of Saint Thomas; they are all pilgrims united by the device of pilgrimage.

The primary identity of about one-third of the pilgrims is established in direct relation to the Church: they have either taken religious vows or derive their income from the Church, or both. This situation reflects, of course, the dominant role of the Church in fourteenth-century society, but a close look at these portraits reveals more than a routine reflection of the makeup of society.

The first of the religious pilgrims to be described is the Prioress. Chaucer's presentation of this religious lady is consistently ironic, and the irony depends chiefly on the disparity between what the Prioress is supposed to be, how she imagines herself, and what in fact she is. Very conspicuous is her inability to understand, to take seriously, or to live by her vows of poverty, chastity, and obedience. And yet she comes across in the *General Prologue* positively, not negatively. But the impression she conveys has nothing to do with her profession of the religious life. She is mindful of clothing, jewelry, courtesy, manners, her own beauty, dead mice, beaten dogs, and the recital of the divine service. Her neglect of her vows and evasion of the rules—minor infractions for the most part—convey Chaucer's sense of her as overly feminine and pretentious and prefigure the larger failure reflected in her tale—her lack of awareness, her lack of true charity, of true mercy. Although her brooch proclaims that love conquers all, her love is a shallow and sentimental love; it is neither for Christ nor for her fellow human beings but for herself.

The official importance of the Prioress is established by her being accompanied by a nun and a priest who are appropriately left undescribed. These attendants—the Nun's Priest and the Second Nun—establish their identity and values in the fictional world of their tales.

The mild discrepancy in the Prioress between the ideal and the actual widens and deepens in the Monk, who expresses outright contempt for his vows—poverty, chastity, obedience, labor, and claustration. The Monk, like the Prioress, comes across strongly in his own self-image: he is worldly, fleshly, and defiant. There is a deliberateness, an insistence about his passion for hunting which suggests, as with the Prioress but more emphatically, a misplaced or misdirected zeal. Utterly inappropriate is his pursuit of the flesh, his rejection of study. Like the Prioress, his religious garb suggests one way of life; his words and actions fly in another direction. Among the more significant details pointing up the discrepancy is Chaucer's comparing the jingling of the bells in his bridle to the ringing of the chapel bell—a reminder of the divine service upon which the Monk has turned his back.

The pilgrim Friar, even more conspicuously than the other religious figures, violates his vows. His is not merely an evasion or a defiance but an abuse of his religious office. Worldly, fleshly, and cunning, he provides a sharp contrast to the founder of his order. Saint Francis, of all the saints, was the Saint who most closely imitated Jesus in his humility, his joyful acceptance of poverty, and in loving and serving his fellow human beings. The Friar, while enjoying all the advantages of belonging to the Order of Brothers, rejects the ideal of service and engages in the odious practice of oppressing the poor in the name of Christ.

In the Friar's offer of "esy penaunce" the penitential theme surfaces and is brought into relationship both with the mercantile theme and the pattern of rivalry. In asserting that he has the power of confession beyond that of a parish priest, Huberd is challenging the Parson in his role as confessor and usurping his primary responsibility for administering the sacrament of Penance. Also, in singling out confession, he has settled on the sacrament which, in practice though not in theory, is the most lucrative. The early mendicants' acceptance of alms freely given in gratitude for service had become by the late fourteenth century in England a complex business operation involving systematic begging. If the sinner makes a donation "unto a povre ordre" (225) this is accepted in lieu of "wepynge and preyeres" (231); the Friar thus becomes an "esy man to yeve penaunce" (223).

His use of the Latin tag *"in principio"* points up especially well his appropriation of religious language for irreligious purposes. When one remembers the opening words of Genesis—"In the beginning God made Heaven and Earth"—and the opening line of the Gospel According to Saint John—"In the beginning was the word"—that is, the echo of the creation of the world in the Old Testament and the doctrine of the Incarnation in the New Testament, *"in principio"* in the mouth of the begging Friar, used as a means of extracting a farthing from a poor widow, provides a bitter contrast:

> For thogh a wydwe hadde noght a sho,
> So plesaunt was his *"In principio,"*
> Yet wolde he have a ferthyng, er he wente.   (253–55)

Although the Friars were licensed to beg and to hear confessions, the way in which the wily Friar combines the two creates a pattern that is subversive of the sacrament of Penance and the authority of the parish priest.

Although the Friar, with his promise of "esy penaunce," was usurping some of the functions that more appropriately belonged to the parish priest, Chaucer does not present the Friar and the Parson as rivals. The Parson remains aloof from the quarreling. In presenting the Friar as engaged in a quarrel with the Summoner, Chaucer reduces the Friar from the level of a man with a religious calling to the level of an avaricious, petty bureaucrat—an absurd one at that.

Chaucer's satirical portrait of the begging Friar with his pleasant speech is reinforced by the begging Friar set in motion in the *Summoner's Tale*. Here the Friar, through the harsher eyes of the Summoner, is especially offensive, boasting of the mendicant ideal of poverty, chastity, and obedience and using it as a cloak for pursuing his own pleasure and enriching himself and his "covent," his brotherhood.

The Prioress, the Monk, and the Friar are religious who have taken vows they fail to understand, respect, and live up to. The Prioress is evasive, the Monk is defiant, the Friar misuses his office. All three essentially serve themselves, not God or their fellow human beings. These three belong to the regular clergy ("regular" from the Latin *regula,* "rule"; "those who follow a rule"). Ironically these "regular" clergy are all irregular; that is, their lives are not regulated by the observance of rules. Equally ironic is the fact that the one member of the secular clergy ("secular" from the Latin *saecula,* "world"; that is, "those who go out into the world"), the Parish Priest, who has gone out into the world, has nevertheless kept his vows and kept himself unspotted.

In a somewhat different category from the three who have taken religious vows and failed to keep them are the two minor functionaries who have taken no vows but who operate in the name of the Church—the Summoner and the Pardoner. The extent to which these petty officials have usurped the role of the religious and by imitating and perverting their techniques, gained power over the people, is a measure of the corruption that existed in the English Church of the fourteenth century. The Summoner is essentially a messenger, employed by the bishop or archbishop who presided over an ecclesiastical court. The Summoner's function was to deliver summonses to persons charged with a variety of offenses—fornication, witchcraft, usury, etc. The accused would be expected to appear at the court to answer charges made against him or her. If found guilty, he or she would be fined and the Summoner paid a percentage of the fine. The inability of the accused to pay might mean arrest or excommunication. The Summoner could practice extortion by playing upon his victims' fear. This profiteering, this cashing in on the imperfections of people was an odious practice. The chief victims were the poor and the ignorant; the rich could bribe themselves free.

Chaucer's Summoner is no routine summons server. He is cunning, unscrupulous, and corrupt. He teaches "a good felawe" (650) not to be in awe of "the erchedekenes curs" (655); that is, the power of the archdeacon to issue excommunications.

Punishment, says he, need take place only in the purse: "Purs is the erchedekenes helle" (658). He is a corrupt rascal whose diseased skin is indicative of his inner corruption; there is no physical remedy for such corruption.

Three aspects of the Pardoner's activities are singled out in the *General Prologue:* his selling of relics, his selling of "pardons," and his preaching—all fraudulent activities. The function of a pardoner, or "questor," as he was officially called, was a limited one as prescribed by canon law: he was a messenger who conveyed indulgences from the Pope or bishop who was authorized to grant them to the person who had fulfilled the conditions necessary to receive them. He was permitted to request alms, which were to be turned over to the proper authorities for the support of such charitable institutions as orphanages and hospitals.

The problem of pardoners abusing their office was an old one by Chaucer's day: as far back as 1215, Pope Innocent III had issued a code for the control of pardoners. They were required to possess a papal or episcopal letter and were permitted only to read this official letter, not to preach. Attempts were made by subsequent popes to control abuses, but the problem persisted. Actually there were two aspects to the problem of regulating pardoners: licensing them and assuring the return of money and goods collected. There were, therefore, two kinds of abuses: authorized questors who diverted the alms collected to their own uses and fraudulent questors who operated with forged credentials. Chaucer's Pardoner practices both kinds of abuse. Moreover, he sells relics. The sale of relics, which had been forbidden by the Lateran Council of 1215, was likewise a practice that proved difficult to control.[1]

One of the details of the Pardoner's striking physical appearance is the "Vernycle" (685), which he has sewn on his cap; that is, a handkerchief bearing the image of Christ's face. In his bag out of sight, but carefully listed in the text, is a pillowcase, which "he seyde was Oure Lady veil" (695). "He seyde"—artfully repeated—he had a piece of the sail of Saint Peter's boat (696–98). "With thise relikes" (701), among them "pigges bones" (700), he got more money in a day than the Parson in two months (703–4).

Of the three activities he engages in, the sale of false relics is

[1]Alfred L. Kellogg, "Chaucer's Satire of the Pardoner," in *Chaucer, Langland, Arthur: Essays in Middle English Literature.* (New Brunswick, N.J.: Rutgers University Press, 1972), pp. 212–44.

the most blatant; the "sale" of false "pardons," the misrepresentation of their efficacy, and the misappropriation of funds all constitute serious abuses, but perhaps the boldest is his usurpation of the priest's functions "in chirche," where he reads from Scripture, sings the Offertory, and preaches (708–14). The Pardoner's skills (like those of the Friar) are verbal: "Wel koude he rede a lessoun or a storie" and best of all "he song an offertorie" (709–10). With his verbal skills and his effrontery, he appropriates the functions of the priest in performing the liturgy and in absolving sinners from Penance.

The Summoner and especially the Pardoner imitate clergymen: the Summoner presuming to "teach" people about excommunication and the Pardoner posing as a "noble ecclesiaste" (708). The Summoner and the Pardoner are minor functionaries and corrupt at that, but it is part of Chaucer's irony that their names suggest the mighty powers of summoning to the divine tribunal and pardoning before the ultimate judge.

In marked contrast to the phony clergymen is the good Parson. Described in the *General Prologue* as "a lerned man, a clerk" (480), he accepts Christ's command to go among the poor and be of service. Combining learning and good works, he goes into the world, putting his learning to the service of his parishioners and using his learning to serve the poor, not to exploit them.

Although one of the chief functions of the parish priest is to offer the sacraments, nothing is said of these in his portrait. In connection with the sacrament of Penance, we think of the Friar's "esy penaunce," and "in chirche" there is the Pardoner. Chaucer stresses the teaching role of the good Parson without, however, referring to the two chief channels of teaching—the pulpit and the confessional. Although in his portrait there is no mention of his administering the sacraments, in his tale he speaks at length on true penitence. In the *General Prologue,* Chaucer emphasizes his preaching the Gospel and especially his exemplifying the virtues of which he speaks. Ironically, this man, whose devotion to the physical and spiritual needs of his parishioners is distinctly unworldly, is the only representative of the secular clergy. This "secular" clergyman who goes out into the world remains a devout and pious man, a dedicated priest, wholly engaged in serving man and God, whereas the "regular" clergy violate their vows and show themselves to be self-interested and worldly, callous, and lacking in dedication.

Although Chaucer's attitude toward his pilgrim-Parson is entirely positive, he has included some details critical of the practices of other priests. This is a good priest, but there are some whose habits are in marked contrast to his. The Parson, Chaucer says, was "ful loath" to excommunicate anyone for not paying his tithes (486). He is unlike the mercenary priests, who flee to St. Paul's to seek "a chaunterie for soules" (507–14), that is, who find it lucrative to say masses for the dead rather than remain in their country parishes to minister to the needs of their parishioners. Chaucer's Parson is "noght a mercenarie" (514); he is free of the spirit of mercantilism that infected so many aspects of the fourteenth-century English Church. The combination in the Parson of learning and devotion to parish duties was exceptional. Even Wyclif, the reformer, for instance, held parish churches while habitually a resident at Oxford.[2]

Throughout most of the pilgrimage, Chaucer's Parson plays an unobtrusive role. He does surface at one point to rebuke the Host for swearing (*MLT,* 1170–77), but emerges most strongly at the end in his prologue and tale.

In the midst of so much falseness, the Parson stands out as the true embodiment of Christian ideals; he not only preaches, that is, uses the language of Christianity, but he lives accordingly. His life is structured in conformity with Christian ideals. He functions in the *General Prologue* and throughout the *Canterbury Tales* as a reminder of what constitutes true Christianity in contrast to so much that is inadequate and false. He makes his way among the worldly, fleshly, and corrupt, issuing his rebukes, preaching his sermons, and, above all, practicing what he preaches.

In his presentation of the pilgrims who are connected to the Church, Chaucer is interested both in the facade of holiness and in true holiness: in the Prioress, who mindlessly uses the trappings of holiness and in the Pardoner and Friar, who deliberately use the facade of holiness to deceive.

The six pilgrims who in the *General Prologue* are most closely connected with religion range from the vain Prioress, the defiant Monk, and wily Friar who is worldly and fleshly but affects a religious pose, the corrupt Summoner and the depraved Pardoner to the devout Parson. As the imperfections of the first five stem from their failures, misrepresentations, and abuses in

---

[2]W. A. Pantin, *The English Church in the Fourteenth Century* (Cambridge: at the University Press, 1955), p. 28

relation to the institution of the church, the goodness of the sixth and last is determined almost wholly in relation to the Gospel.

Besides these six religious pilgrims who are described in the *General Prologue,* there are two who accompany the Prioress—a nun and a priest. All eight tell tales. There is one other religious figure, a canon who joins the pilgrimage briefly and who exists chiefly in the tale his yeoman tells.

About one-third of the pilgrims have either taken religious vows or are associated with the organization of the Church. The other pilgrims making their way to Canterbury, although not deriving their livelihoods from the Church, are all Christian folk. The fact that they are on a pilgrimage serves as a reminder that they are products of a Christian society, exist in a religious context, and form part of a framework of religious values.

They are, however, not only a part of the religious framework, they exist in the immediate impact they have on the reader—and this emerges through the language that Chaucer the narrator uses and they themselves use, and this language is often explicitly Christian.

They are all pilgrims, the Wife of Bath, the Shipman, the Miller, and all the others. In the Miller, a pugilist, cheat and teller of ribald tales, Chaucer creates one of a number of instances of unredeemed humanity; to him, life—and the pilgrimage—is all pleasure and in no sense penitential. Like many another rascal, he is somewhat redeemed in the generous art of his creator by the brilliant tale he tells. As everyone knows, it is a bawdy story; what is perhaps less well known is that it is very rich in religious language. Although the uses to which this language is put are hardly devotional, the structure of the tale—the exposure and punishment of folly—is not inconsistent with a broadly conceived religious view.

There are in the *Canterbury Tales* two levels of characters: those whom Chaucer presents as fellow pilgrims and contemporaries and those who appear in the fictional world of the tales. Some of the stories the pilgrims tell reflect the fourteenth-century world, but quite often the fictional world extends to earlier times and distant places—pagan Greece, early Britain, ancient Rome. In some of the tales, the differentiation is almost complete; in others there are a juxtaposing and blending of Christian and pagan customs, terminology, values, and behavior. These excursions into fictional space and time provide Chaucer and his audience with a temporary and imaginative escape from their all-too "Christian" world with its bishops, sacraments, statues of the Virgin, crucifixes, and the like.

The characters in the tales range even more widely than the pilgrims: there are good pagans, that is, those who are placed in a pagan setting but who use language, respond to values, and exemplify ideals that are to some extent Christian; there are exemplary Christians, especially from earlier times; and there are pagans and Christians who are treacherous and murderous.

Some of the tales are set in England—where the characters seem virtually indistinguishable from the pilgrim characters. The difference is that these characters are caught up in a plot structure, as distinct from the pilgrimage structure, and although the language is Chaucer's, they are presented from the point of view of another pilgrim. For instance, the summoner in the *Friar's Tale* is virtually indistinguishable from the pilgrim-Summoner, but he is set in motion, put into a plot-structure, and given language by Chaucer's pilgrim-Friar. Similarly, the friar in the *Summoner's Tale*.

The chief action of the pilgrims is their movement toward Canterbury; in the links and the exchanges of tales they interact with each other in almost exclusively verbal terms. The characters in the tales, however, are involved in actions: they are placed in situations, and they succeed or fail; there are outcomes, consequences; rewards, punishments, or transformations; in short, there are structures.

All the characters in the imaginative world of the *Canterbury Tales*—the pilgrims and the characters in the tales—exist in the context of the pilgrimage. But the characters in the tales are involved in separate structures, apart from the structure of pilgrimage. Like the pilgrims, the characters in the tales range from exemplary to rascally. The good Parson has no exact counterpart in the tales, but some of the virtues he possesses appear personified in Custance and Griselda, the exemplary heroines of the tales told by the Man of Law and the Clerk, heroines who are tested and prove their worth. Whereas we are told that the Parson is patient and devout, these heroines exemplify these qualities in the plot structure. The Parson alone does not project an imaginative structure; his "tale" is a treatise.

One of the basic structures is the test, which is both a religious and a folktale pattern. In the tales of the Man of Law and the

Clerk, both Custance and Griselda are tested, prove their worth, and are rewarded. Here religious language and structure support each other. These learned men tell tales that convey an image of heroines of long ago and far away—women who conform to their notions of holiness and virtue.

The worst rascals among the "religious" pilgrims project the worst rascals in their tales: the wily Friar tells of a scoundrel-summoner; the rascally Summoner tells of an absurdly phony friar. The structure of the pilgrim-Friar's tale follows the pattern of vice-punished; it enables him to punish both the fictitious and pilgrim Summoner. And similarly the pilgrim-Summoner gets revenge on both the fictitious and the pilgrim-Friar. The self-centered and unscrupulous Pardoner follows up the exhibition of his fraudulent practices in his prologue with a tale that is an imaginative projection of deception, betrayal, and death in which three brothers-who-would-slay-death slay each other.

A religious phenomenon of considerable interest is the sinner who repents. Although there are numerous references to repentance in the *Canterbury Tales* (in the tales of the Friar, Pardoner, and Parson, especially), there are no instances on the pilgrimage, and actual repentance is not even common in the fictional world of the tales.

A pattern closely related to the repentant sinner is religious conversion—in the explicitly religious tales, conversion from paganism to Christianity. The tales in which conversions take place—the Man of Law's and the Second Nun's—are interestingly enough set in earlier times. Conversion in the tales is a simple occurrence, a matter of statement. The actual process of change from sinfulness to holiness is not represented.

The characters in the tales—as well as the pilgrims—exist in a religious context ranging from the Christian (though irreligious) fourteenth century to the surprisingly Christian world of the pagan past. Thus, through the use of different cultural settings and the introduction of both exemplary and depraved characters, Chaucer explores a variety of value systems in the fictional world of his *Canterbury Tales*.

Among the explicitly Christian tales are those of the Prioress, the Second Nun, the Clerk, the Man of Law, Chaucer's own tale of Melibeus, and the final "tale" of the Canterbury pilgrimage, the Parson's treatise on penitence and the seven deadly sins.

There are other tales in which a great deal of explicitly Christian language is used, but the context is anything but religious. Here the structure may serve a religious purpose, but it functions differently from the straight Christian tales; instead of exemplifying virtue, these tales mock vice and folly and expose fraud and hence have a cleansing, purging effect. They may be humorous, even bawdy; they may be told in a spirit of mockery or even malice, but the structure serves a moral purpose and insofar as morality is a component of religion, they serve a religious purpose. Among these are the tales of the Friar and the Summoner and the *Nun's Priest's Tale*.

A third type of religious tale is, like the first group, serious, but like the second, aimed at the exposure of vice; the best example of this is the *Pardoner's Tale*.

Belonging to a special group are several tales that deal essentially with virtuous actions but are not explicitly Christian; they may, like the *Knight's Tale*, have pagan settings and pagan religious elements that are, however, similar to those in the Christian tales.

What remains are the fabliaux—the tales of the Miller, the Reeve, the Shipman, and the Merchant. Essentially entertainment, all involve sex and tricks. They too are permeated by religious references, for the most part explicitly Christian, but the effect of the religious language in inappropriate contexts is hilarious.

Of the twenty-odd tales, all contain religious language, and analysis will, I believe, show that all are structured so as to support a religious or moral position. One might then ask why Chaucer at the end of his work found it necessary to revoke "the tales of Caunterbury, thilke sownen into synne" (1085). The answer, I think, is that many of the religious references, especially in the fabliaux, occur in contexts that may seem blasphemous. And there is no doubt that as an artist Chaucer was not deeply engaged in his virtuous figures but was, and knew that he was, deeply involved in creating the challengers to orthodoxy, like the Wife of Bath, and the hilarious impieties of his grosser characters. Although Chaucer did not finally support the view that sexy and tricky people will prevail, he did create for them and vicariously share with them their moments of glory.

Throughout the *Canterbury Tales* Chaucer balances religious and profane elements: piety and impiety, reverence and irreverence, sincere religious devotion and the satirical use of religious forms. In varying combinations he juxtaposes and blends pagan and Christian language and values, contrasting and weighing possibilities and consequences. There are the limited good of the *Knight's Tale,* the ugly vision of the *Merchant's Tale,* the bright world of the *Franklin's Tale.*

The continuous use of religious references serves as a reminder that the pilgrimage is not merely a social or literary venture; these references function as reminders of the spiritual possibilities of pilgrimage. Chaucer moves toward the end of the *Canterbury Tales* closer to exclusively Christian concerns. In placing the *Parson's Tale* and his own *Retraction* last, he sets the whole work in a Christian perspective.

Chaucer is not primarily a religious poet, as Dante and Langland are. But he is a great and original poet whose viewpoint is essentially Christian. For many of his richest and most characteristic effects he uses religious language, and throughout the *Canterbury Tales* he uses religious structures—in the tales and in the pilgrimage itself. In the end, the language and the structures are Chaucer's.

BIBLIOGRAPHIC NOTE

The following books and articles, in addition to those listed in the footnotes, contain valuable information and insights on religion in Chaucer.

Baldwin, Ralph. *The Unity of the Canterbury Tales, Anglistica* (Copenhagen), 5, 1955). Excerpts reprinted in *Chaucer Criticism: The Canterbury Tales,* Richard Schoeck and Jerome Taylor, eds. (Notre Dame, Ind.: University of Notre Dame Press, 1960), pp. 14–51.

Birney, Earle. "After His Ymage: the Central Ironies of the Friar's Tale," *Mediaeval Studies* (Toronto), 21 (1959), 17–35.

Block, Edward A. "Originality, Controlling Purpose, and Craftsmanship in Chaucer's Man of Law's Tale," *Publications of the Modern Language Association,* 68 (1953), 572–616.

Boyd, Beverly. *Chaucer and the Liturgy* (Philadelphia: Dorrance, 1967).

Chapman, C. O. "Chaucer on Preachers and Preaching," *Publi-*

cations of the Modern Language Association, 44 (1929), 178–85.

Du Boulay, F. R. H. *An Age of Ambition: English Society in the Late Middle Ages* (London: Nelson, 1970), Chap. 8.

Gordon, James D. "Chaucer's Retraction: A Review of Opinion," in *Studies in Medieval Literature in Honor of Professor Albert Croll Baugh* (Philadelphia: University of Pennsylvania Press, 1961), pp. 81–96.

Hall, Donald John. *English Mediaeval Pilgrimage* (London: Routledge and Kegan Paul, 1966).

Harder, Kelsie B. "Chaucer's Use of the Mystery Plays in the Miller's Tale," *Modern Language Quarterly,* 17 (1956), 193–98.

Kaske, R. E. "The *Canticum Canticorum* in the Miller's Tale," *Studies in Philology,* 59 (1962), 479–500.

Landrum, Grace W. "Chaucer's Use of the Vulgate," *Publications of the Modern Language Association,* 39 (1924), 75–100.

Levy, Bernard S. "Biblical Parody in the Summoner's Tale," *Tennessee Studies in Literature,* 11 (1966), 45–60.

Lumiansky, R. M. "Chaucer's Retraction and the Degree of Completeness of the *Canterbury Tales,*" *Tulane Studies in English,* 6 (1956), 5–13.

Makarewicz, Sister Mary Raynelda. *The Patristic Influence on Chaucer* (Washington: Catholic University of America Press, 1953).

McNamara, John. "Chaucer's Use of the Epistle of St. James in the Clerk's Tale," *The Chaucer Review,* 7 (1973), 184–93.

Merrill, Thomas F. "Wrath and Rhetoric in the Summoner's Tale," *Texas Studies in Literature and Language,* 4 (1962), 341–50.

Miller, Clarence H. and Roberta Bux Bosse. "Chaucer's Pardoner and the Mass," *The Chaucer Review,* 6 (1972), 171–84.

Mroczkowski, Premyslaw. "The Friar's Tale and its Pulpit Background," *English Studies Today,* G. A. Bonnard, ed., 2 (1961), 107–20.

Owen, Charles A., Jr. "The Development of the *Canterbury Tales,*" *Journal of English and Germanic Philology,* 57 (1958), 449–76.

Ruggiers, Paul. *The Art of the Canterbury Tales* (Madison, Wisc.: University of Wisconsin, 1965).

Ryan, Lawrence, V. "The Canon's Yeoman's Desperate Confession," *The Chaucer Review,* 8 (1974), 297–310.

Sayce, Olive. "Chaucer's 'Retractions': The Conclusion of the *Canterbury Tales* and Its Place in Literary Tradition," *Medium Aevum,* 40 (1971), 230–48.

Shain, Charles E. "Pulpit Rhetoric in Three Canterbury Tales," *Modern Language Notes,* 70 (1955), 235–45.

Thomas, Mary Edith. *Medieval Skepticism and Chaucer* (New York: The William-Frederick Press, 1950).

Thompson, W. Meredith. "Chaucer's Translation of the Bible," in *English and Medieval Studies Presented to J. R. R. Tolkien,* Norman Davis and C. L. Wrenn, eds. (London: Allen and Unwin, 1962), pp. 183–99.

Turner, Arthur W. "Biblical Women in *The Merchant's Tale* and *The Tale of Melibee,*" *English Language Notes,* 3 (1965), 92–95.

Williams, Arnold. "Chaucer and the Friars," *Speculum,* 28 (1953), 499–513.

———. "The 'Limitour' of Chaucer's Time and his 'Limitacioun,' " *Studies in Philology,* 57 (1960), 463–78.

Yunck, John A. "Religious Elements in Chaucer's *Man of Law's Tale,*" *ELH, A Journal of English Literary History,* 27 (1960), 249–61.

Winthrop Wetherbee

Some Intellectual Themes in Chaucer's Poetry

Learning and didacticism were fundamental elements in the medieval conception of serious poetry, and both are present in abundance in the poetry of Chaucer. He was probably the most learned of medieval English poets, and, though he offers nothing like Langland's intimacy with the habits and themes of contemporary scholasticism or the homiletic intricacies and discourses on political philosophy of Gower, he is also in many ways the most intellectual. His intellectualism appears not only in the range of his learning but in its particularity: in the penetration and precision with which he locates and probes the issues raised by the most complex of earlier poetry, in his frequent citation and deep knowledge of his preferred "old books," but also in the rigor with which he defines the limits of his acceptance of their authority. It is present in his acute awareness of the implications of his development as a poet and of the risks involved in committing himself to this medium, which was capable of yielding insights inaccessible to philosophy or theology, but which by its very independent status was denied the legitimacy of the knowledge attained through these disciplines. As his poetry evolves, and most decisively in the *Canterbury Tales,* this concern becomes merged with the larger question of human self-determination in general and helps to reveal Chaucer's response to such major issues in fourteenth-century thought as the bases and abuses of civil and ecclesiastical authority, the limits of human freedom, and the implications of will and character.

That Chaucer was thoroughly at home with the details of court ceremonial, law, and business is understandable in the light of his career as a courtier-diplomat and later as a well-to-do civil servant. But he also possessed a detailed knowledge of medicine, astrology, astronomy, and, apparently, alchemy, and uses this knowledge as he uses his keen eye for physical detail to illumine the lives and natures of his characters. Though the extent to which a person's horoscope, physical type, or temperament determined his character and actions was a question much debated in his time, his use of such detail, which can be explained by reference to standard medieval texts, is always enriching and often essential to a correct interpretation. To know, for example, that several of the physical traits assigned to the Summoner would probably have been recognized as symptoms of debauchery, while the Pardoner's would have indicated a congenital ailment, rightly conditions our response to them. Again, a commitment to pursuits whose validity was disputed, such as the Canon's alchemy or the fatalistic reading of the stars which the Man of Law interpolates with his affirmations of God's providence, will have a psychological and moral significance, suggesting a doubt or neglect of spiritual values or a will to exploit nature and science for selfish reasons. In any case, it is important to recognize that from that first essay in pseudo-physics with which the Eagle explains to "Geffrey" the gravitation of all sound toward the House of Fame, all such precise instances of Chaucer's scientific range, competence and frequent virtuosity must be considered as thematic elements in the larger contexts of his poetry.

As is made plain elsewhere in this volume, Chaucer's knowledge of European poetry in Latin and the Romance vernaculars was as exceptional in its extent and depth as his learning in general, and from the beginning his sense of poetic vocation involved the ambition to make English poetry intellectually respectable in comparison with that of France and Italy. He is the first Englishman to have made a major contribution to what may be called the intellectual tradition in medieval poetry, a tradition which begins with the philosophical allegories and often highly cerebral love lyrics of the Latin poets of the twelfth-century schools and of which the great vernacular example was Jean de Meun's portion of the *Roman de la Rose*. It was from this tradition that Chaucer derived the forms and major themes of his early poetry, and it will be worthwhile to look briefly at its history.

The twelfth century saw a great renewal of contact with classical culture and a newly active interest in philosophy and science. The cosmological portions of Plato's *Timaeus* (the only work of Plato, apart from quotations in later authors, known in the West at this period) provided a rudimentary paradigm of the order of the universe, a "model" in C. S. Lewis's phrase, and a starting point for scientific investigation of the nature of things. The cosmology of the Stoics, as conveyed by Seneca and in the *De natura deorum* ("On the Nature of the Gods") of Cicero, and a simplified version of Hermetic and neo-Platonist cosmology drawn from Apuleius and the late-Latin encyclopedists Macrobius and Martianus Capella were adapted to this framework, and these several influences collaborated to inspire a view of the universe as a manifestation of God, its order and perpetual life reflecting his wisdom and bounty. Together with the rudiments of medicine, psychology, and astrology, which were becoming known through translation and adaptation of Arabic texts, they provoked a new concern with the place of humanity in the scheme of things and the extent to which its physical and psychological life was subject to the influence of the divine *causae* operating in nature at large. New questions were raised about the implications of imagination and intuition and the bases of knowledge and morality. One important result of these concerns was a newly optimistic view of the human condition and of humanity's capacity for achieving rational and potentially spiritual orientation through cooperation with the natural order.

These concerns provided a starting point for the work of a group of poets whose writings are in many ways the most influential achievement of the "twelfth-century renaissance." The *Cosmographia* of Bernardus Silvestris and the *De planctu naturae* ("Nature's Complaint") of Alain de Lille are philosophical allegories in which humanity's relation with the universe is explored and the power of *Natura* to sustain and discipline its life set against the pressure of humanity's corrupted will and passions, which tend toward self-destruction. Both poets offer a vivid picture of the problem itself, and neither attempts a decisive resolution: Nature's appeal to humanity and her larger "yearning" for the fulfillment of perfect order, as well as the expression of humanity's own doubts, confusions, and aspirations, are left in suspense, voices whose dialogue is halting and at times almost abortive. But at the same time both express a lofty humanism, emphasizing the potential dignity of a human nature restored to creative harmony with the larger natural order.

Similar preoccupations characterize many of the best Latin love lyrics of the period, notably certain poems of Walter of Chatillon and a number of the anonymous masterpieces of the *Carmina Burana*. These deal with love largely in terms of the contradictory feelings it arouses and the contingency of the ebbs and flows of feeling on processes seemingly beyond human control. Making a free use of philosophical terminology and frequently drawing on twelfth-century science to characterize the lover's subjection to larger forces, these poets regard humanity's cosmic affinities and the intuition of an ordering of human emotion by the therapeutic influence of nature with a certain ambivalence, anxious to find a stable basis for evaluating the experience of love, but fearful that the potential harmony they intuit is a mere pathetic fallacy. The same concern with irresolution and paradox characterizes many of the debate poems and learned satires of the time; these often exploit the contradictory implications of classical myth, in which, as interpreted by medieval mythographers, the gods could be seen now as symbols of cosmic harmony, now as exemplars of passion and conflict, to expose the contradictory implications of humanity's situation in the universe.

Despite the emphasis of these poets on the uncertainties of the human condition, their work is finally deeply humanistic in intention. But while they had great influence, the tentative nature of their affirmation of the capacities of humanity, and the rudimentary state of the cosmology and psychology which provided its context, left their idealism vulnerable to the criticism of later and more sophisticated poets. The limitations of their vision are brilliantly exposed in the continuation by the thirteenth-century French poet Jean de Meun of the *Roman de la Rose* of Guillaume de Lorris. Jean transfers Guillaume's courtly dream vision, a graceful and intricate allegory of the process of falling in love, to a context which is basically that of twelfth-century philosophical allegory, complicated by Jean's own extended forays into science, mythology, and social satire. His narrative traces the long progression from the lover's initial subjection to *Amors* to his conquest and impregnation of his Rose at the instigation of Venus, and, as it proceeds, Reason and Nature, as well as Venus, seek to influence his actions. Each provides an elaborate philosophical justification for her insistence on procreation as love's proper end, and each conceives her vision of rightly ordered love as involving a transcendence of the irrational and self-interested love associated with Venus. In the end the appeals of both Reason and Nature are rewarded, as the lover fulfills Nature's commandment and achieves the rationally appropriate goal of procreation; but this goal is achieved by means which confound any attempt at philosophical justification and wholly subvert the ostensible purpose of Jean's allegorical setting. For the lover's goal is achieved by the most complex and devious means, through treachery, hypocrisy, and finally the violence of simple lust. The very figures who are the objects of Jean's most scathing satire, embodiments of the corruption of society and the Church, are the go-betweens who bring the lover within range of his object; and he explicitly repudiates Reason, even as he obeys her dictates, in the moment of his final conquest.

Given the paramount importance of Jean de Meun as an influence on Chaucer's poetry, it is striking that in his handling of their common sources in the Latin tradition, he seems to have taken Jean's largely subversive use of these sources as by no means the definitive treatment of their themes and concerns. It is true, of course, as the *Canterbury Tales* above all serve to indicate, that he was fully aware, perhaps more aware than any later poet, of the philosophical implications of Jean's skepticism about the idealistic tendencies of the Latin tradition and his subversive use of social realism; but at the same time, though capable of a skepticism as profound as Jean's, he was distrustful of this very capacity in himself and deeply sympathetic with the intuitions of a potential fulfillment in nature which had led the Latin poets to dwell so insistently on the tensions in human experience. No vernacular poem provides so sympathetic a recreation of the atmosphere of this poetry as Chaucer's *Parliament of Fowls,* where cosmic allegory, debate, and lyric contribute together to the search for a harmonious means of entry into the experience of love. Like the Latin poems, the *Parliament* focuses on contradiction: the complex experience of a garden which encompasses both the Temple of Venus, with its grim images of love exploited, degraded, and destroyed, and the beautifully evoked ritual of procreation under the presiding authority of the goddess Nature. Chaucer seems to set his desire to share the tentatively affirmative attitude of the Latin allegorists against a recognition like Jean's of the many forces which work to resist the fulfillment of love; the poem ends with the debate unresolved, but the possibility of affirmation is left open.

A similar opposition may be seen in the *Troilus and Criseyde,* where the almost religious idealism of Troilus is juxtaposed with the pragmatic materialism of Pandarus. Like the cynical schemers who aid the lover of the *Roman de la Rose* in his pursuit of the Rose, Pandarus's machinations both serve Troilus's love and threaten to degrade it; but again, as in the *Parliament,* Chaucer refuses to make any final concession to pragmatism. His Troilus is sustained by an idealizing vision to which tactical skill bears only a contingent relation and which is essentially that of the Latin tradition. As his love approaches fulfillment, he sees it as participating in a larger love, the "holy bond of things" which governs all created life as well as the hearts of human beings. The poet himself uses similarly comprehensive language in an invocation of love which preludes this fulfillment:

> In hevene and helle, in erthe and salte see
> Is felt thi myght, if that I wel descerne;
> As man, brid, best, fissh, herbe, and grene tree
> Thee fele in tymes with vapour eterne.
> God loveth, and to love wol nought werne;
> And in this world no lyves creature
> Withouten love is worth, or may endure.   (3.8–14)

How Troilus's idealism survives the betrayal of his love on the earthly plane is a question which, on one level, is beyond the scope of this essay: it involves Chaucer's coming to terms with the supremely challenging example of Dante, and while it leads to a profound affirmation of the meaning of love, this affirmation depends on intuitions in which poetic insight verges on religion. At the same time it has a more strictly philosophical aspect: after his death in battle and before being translated to the realm of the shades, Troilus's spirit is brought to the outer limit of the universe, and from this symbolic vantage point granted a brief glimpse into the nature of things; he realizes that his love, like all earthly joys, was doomed by its lack of true orientation, and learns to contemn not only his own former folly but

> al oure work that foloweth so
> The blynde lust, the which that may nat laste.   (5.1823–24)

Chaucer proceeds in the poem's magnificent conclusion to show that for Christians there is another possible attitude, both more sympathetic and more decisively transcendent; but Troilus's final insight nonetheless expresses an attitude which was important to the poet and which brings us into contact with one of the deepest of his intellectual obligations. In addition to the philosophical poets of the twelfth century and largely through his assimilation of their intellectual concerns, Chaucer knew well a group of late-classical authors who played an important role in transmitting ancient thought and learning to the medieval world. In the austere neo-Platonism common to these authors, who include the encyclopedists Macrobius and Martianus Capella and the philosopher-statesman Boethius, Chaucer found a foil to the development of a number of his own characteristic attitudes, and Boethius's masterpiece, *The Consolation of Philosophy,* probably affected his thought more than any other single work.

Macrobius's commentary on the *Somnium Scipionis* ("Scipio's Dream") of Cicero interprets the stern philosophy of Cicero's visionary fragment, in which the mission of the statesman is presented as a vocation demanding total dedication to the common good and a denial of earthly desires in the interest of one's immortal soul, in the light of the commentator's own neo-Platonism, and was, in addition, a major source of medieval dream-theory of the sort with which Chaucer flirts so tantalizingly but so indecisively in his early poems. Martianus's *Marriage of Philology and Mercury,* an extremely influential manual of the seven liberal arts, is prefaced by an elaborate allegory illustrating the capacity of Philology, or learning, wedded to Mercury, representing divinely inspired eloquence, to bring the human mind to an awareness of its transcendent origins and destiny. The allegory culminates in Philology's apotheosis and ascent to heaven, where the marriage is performed, and this motif, together with the similar spiritual ascent in the *Somnium Scipionis,* inspired the celestial journeys which are central motifs in the *Cosmographia* of Bernardus Silvestris and Alain de Lille's *Anticlaudianus.* Chaucer draws on both as well as on Alain in constructing his *House of Fame,* where the journey motif is treated half parodically; the poem may be seen as a quest for the source of poetic themes and inspiration, hindered in Chaucer's case by the poet's inability to transcend his preoccupation with earthly love and poetic fable. "Philology" is reduced to a host of conflicting traditions and motifs, and eloquence dissolves into a babel of rumors and half-truths. Instead of realizing a marriage between the two, the poet is shown the impossibility of establishing poetry on a basis of certain knowledge, an important anticipation of the way in which "reality" is handled in the *Canterbury Tales.*

A summary of the *Somnium Scipionis* provides the cosmic

backdrop for the vision of the *Parliament of Fowls,* and it is perhaps also the ultimate source of the passage appropriated from Boccaccio's *Teseida* to describe Troilus's moment of posthumous enlightenment discussed above. There can be no doubt that Chaucer respected the high standard set for intellectual and moral life in this work and was provoked by the consonance with Christian thought of its strong note of *contemptus mundi*. At the same time, his use of the *Somnium Scipionis* in the *Parliament* is such as to suggest that he found its repudiation of earthly things too extreme: as Martianus's marriage of learning and eloquence seems to exclude most of the material with which the poet must inevitably deal, Macrobius's vision seems to bear no functional relation to the search for a satisfactory approach to love which is the poem's main concern. It seems to afford no place for merely human desire and presents the cosmic order as a standard by which all but the most saintly of human beings stand condemned. There seems to be no alternative to a contaminating involvement with the world on the one hand and total withdrawal on the other—the sort of withdrawal which Troilus achieves only in death.

I think a recognition of this problem may help us to explain the tremendous importance of Boethius in Chaucer's thought, for Boethius is at once rigorous in his definition of the mission of philosophy and acutely sensitive to the problems which its demands create on the level of experience. The *Consolation,* a dialogue between a prisoner and the preceptress of his youth, Philosophy, is grounded in real experience: the author, a patrician drawn by a deep sense of noblesse oblige to devote his life to public affairs and the preservation of learning in sixth-century Italy, had been imprisoned on highly questionable grounds of treason, conspiracy, and sacrilege and was eventually to be executed. His sense of wrong and his need to attain a rational view of his situation must have been equally great and help to explain why the process of his withdrawal from a preoccupation with his own misfortunes to a growing recognition of the contingency of happiness on a belief in God's providence is punctuated by expressions of doubt, dissent, and frustration.

Boethius is led by Philosophy to acknowledge rationally that anxiety attends all mere earthly happiness, so that the loss of such happiness is not to be mourned; that the injustice he sees around him is only apparent, since the wicked are punished by their own wickedness and the good rewarded by the testing and vindication of their virtue; and that the foreseeing providence of God which ensures this is thus able to make all fortune serve its ends. But the difficulty of keeping this providential order firmly in mind when one is continually confronted by cases in which joy and sorrow seem to be distributed at random is a problem which nags the dreamer even after he has learned the difficult lesson of accepting his own misfortunes. Moreover, if the randomness of things is denied, does the acceptance of an all-disposing providence leave room for human freedom? If all is foreseen and foreordained, virtue seems meaningless and providence a kind of slavery. This is, of course, a fundamental issue in Christian thought, and Philosophy's answer is a classic statement on the problem: God foresees events which nonetheless come to pass through the free exercise of human will: all time is a constant present to Him, "and the eternal present of His vision concurs with the future character of our actions, distributing rewards to the good and punishments to the evil (Book 5, Prose 6, p. 119, Green translation)." Thus virtue has meaning, and prayers rightly offered are not in vain.

On this note the *Consolation* ends, the prisoner having made no further contribution to the dialogue and Philosophy, in effect, having given way to religion. But the final effect of the dialogue as a whole involves more than a recognition of the majestic unfolding of Philosophy's argument. The prisoner's participation serves to dramatize at once the urgency and the difficulty of adhering to Philosophy's teachings and so compels us to experience the dialogue on two levels. Philosophy employs a number of hortatory *exempla,* short poems on renunciation and perseverance illustrated by mythical figures: Orpheus and Eurydice, the labors of Hercules, Agamemnon and Iphigenia at Aulis. In the context of the prisoner's situation these *exempla* assume an added dimension, reminding us of the painful and potentially tragic burden which the search for the *via recta* imposes.

It seems to have been this human element in the *Consolation* which appealed to Chaucer, for whom Boethius is the embodiment of moral seriousness, and his own use of Boethius's teachings is intimately bound up with the experience of his characters. There is a sustained and largely ironic parallel between the structure of the *Consolation* and that of the *Troilus*. In each work the hero is introduced to an experience which brings out his inherent idealism: as Troilus's experience climaxes in the consummation of a love which seems to participate in the divine harmony,

Boethius is led to a vision of the universe as pervaded and sustained by God's benevolence in the central portions of the *Consolation*. But in both cases this climactic experience is only the midpoint on a line which leads to an engagement with new problems. Troilus, after his separation from Criseyde, is led to review his situation in terms of just those questions about free will and determinism which vex Boethius in the later books of the *Consolation,* and though the pressure of subjective feeling inhibits his understanding, he is, after death, "consoled" by a vision of the blindness and misery of the world in comparison with the felicity implicit in the larger order of things. But there is a hint of bitterness and self-mockery in Troilus's laughter in this final moment which suggests that such philosophy has left the finest elements of his nature unfulfilled and which provides a foil to the religious perspective with which the poem concludes.

Before considering the intellectual context of the *Canterbury Tales* in general, it is worth reviewing the broad character of the intellectual engagements dramatized in Chaucer's earlier poems. Consistently, I think, we may see Chaucer using his sources in a way which tests the existential implications of their ideas, their accessibility and value for people immersed in the world of experience. If Martianus Capella is recalled in the *House of Fame,* it is to show ironically the problems involved in bringing poetry and learning into a fulfilling harmony. In the *Parliament,* Macrobius, Jean de Meun, and the twelfth-century allegorists are set in an opposition which ends in an impasse, so deeply contradictory are their views on the place and value of love in the order of things. Troilus, a victim in his earthly life of a fatal inability to gain a true perspective on the love whose larger implications he nonetheless intuits and affirms, who is a lover and a poet but can become a philosopher only in death, lives out the implications of the opposition dramatized in the *Parliament.* Even as his poetry evolves away from the inherited forms of French and Latin allegory, Chaucer continues to employ their materials and techniques in dealing with the intellectual aspects of his themes, setting the concrete experience of love and suffering in the framework of that cosmology which the neo-Platonists had imbued with fundamental moral values and which thus constitutes the arena within which these values are applied, successfully or unsuccessfully, to life.

The *Knight's Tale* may be seen to dramatize a synthesizing of Chaucer's philosophical values as a prelude to the testing of these values in the lives and attitudes of the Canterbury pilgrims. As in the *Troilus,* the structure itself may be called "Boethian," for the implications of the action steadily expand from an initial focusing on the fortunes of war and love to the point at which, with Arcite's death at the hands of the gods, human life seems to be at the mercy of a complex of destructive powers; as in the *Roman de la Rose,* the implications of order presented by the poem's form are set against a conspiracy of subversive agents, but here the atmosphere is far more intense. The ironic relationship of Mars, Diana, and Venus, whose intervention in the action constitutes both an acknowledgment and a thwarting of their authority and the prayers of their human servants, is in stark contrast to the comic convergence of the authority of Nature, Reason, and Venus in the denouement of the *Roman.* In the poem's somber and moving conclusion, Boethian *contemptus mundi* and Boethian affirmation are brought together. First Egeus expresses the stern lesson which the events of the poem have conspired to teach:

> This world nys but a thurghfare ful of wo,
> And we been pilgrymes, passynge to and fro.
> Deeth is an ende of every worldly soore.   (*KnT*, 2847–49)

Then Theseus assumes the responsibility of his office in the world of the poem and offers the concluding reaffirmation of the benevolence which governs all things. The dignity and beauty of his speech temper our knowledge that such philosophical optimism is the sole bulwark left to the Athenians against the pressure of despair and that nameless terror which lurks beneath the powerful account of Arcite's funeral.

In the *Knight's Tale* the challenge posed by the tragic possibilities of life to the ordering and affirming power of philosophy is clearly indicated. In general Chaucer's handling of ideas in the *Canterbury Tales* is far more oblique. There is, of course, much discussion of such topics as marriage, honor, and justice, but its context is, for the most part, the traditions of homiletics and hagiography and the literature of *courtoisie* rather than philosophy and philosophical poetry. The large questions of providence, necessity, and free will are raised at a number of points, but they are refracted through personalities so diverse as the Man of Law, the Nun's Priest, and the Franklin's Dorigen.

The relation of the *Tales* to Chaucer's intellectual concerns is closely bound up with the way in which they constitute a development away from his earlier poetry. In the course of his dealings with Boethius' orchestration of rational conviction and existential doubt and with the challenging opposition between idealist and pragmatic views of the place of love, he had learned not to seek final answers to philosophical questions but to regard poetry as a medium within which ideas and attitudes had to be viewed, as it were, in suspension; in the *Canterbury Tales* this conception of the function of poetry is put to the test. Chaucer chooses as his setting a society in transition and lets all values express themselves through characters whose attitudes often confound idealism and materialism in such a way as to deliberately thwart the ordering influence of the traditional modes in which he had written previously. In the process he meets head on the challenge of Jean de Meun, employing a realism at least as radical as Jean's yet refusing, I think, to acquiesce in the too simply reductive implication which such realism seems to bear in the *Roman*.

But while Jean is obviously a major presence in the *Tales,* the poem's contemporary setting and the obviously topical concerns of many characters also raise the question of Chaucer's relation to the intellectual currents of his own place and time, and consideration of these may help to account for a number of characteristic features of the work. Chaucer's social conservatism and deliberate de-emphasis of the explicitly philosophical concerns of his earlier poems make it difficult to posit any too direct influence from contemporary thought, but his responsiveness to questions which engaged the philosophers of his day appears in a number of ways.

In the area of social thought, the most influential thinker of the period was John Wyclif, whom Chaucer may conceivably have known in his heyday, since both men received the patronage of John of Gaunt. The theme of his major works is the problem of abuses in government and particularly the government of the Church. He declared that all earthly dominion is owed to God's grace, that a prelate who abused his authority should be removed from office, and that the government of the Church did not depend on the existence of a papacy and cardinalate. His influence was greatly hindered by a suspicion that his ideas had helped to incite the Peasants' Revolt of 1381, but he was accepted as no more than a highly controversial theologian during the earlier stages of his career: his views on church government were challenged by Ralph Strode, the Oxford theologian to whom, with

John Gower, Chaucer later offered his *Troilus* for correction, but it seems clear that the debate was conducted on terms of mutual respect.

In general, on the level of practical politics, Chaucer seems to have been fundamentally conservative in his attitude toward established authority in Church and state. He nowhere addresses the condition of the episcopal hierarchy and never seems to hint at any reform more radical than the renewal of Christian values urged in the *Parson's Tale*. On the social plane his criticism is somewhat more analytical: he is clearly troubled by a growing commercialism in social relations and by the fact that shifting relations among the classes of society have led to a general restlessness, widespread ambition, and a concern with "maistrye" which appears in a thousand forms. But where social change is mentioned, as in Chaucer's allusions to the Peasants' Revolt, it is disparaged, and his own concern seems consistently to be due to the decline of established values rather than the need for new ones.

At the same time, it is clear from his treatment of the Pardoner and Friar, particularly as contrasted with the Parson and the Nun's Priest, that he shares Langland's sense of the pervasive demoralization at work in the church at large, and that a central issue in his criticism, as in Wyclif's, is the abuse of authority. He sees that such a man as the Friar, who has lost all vital awareness of the spiritual function of his office, constitutes a positive obstacle to the spiritual good of the community. And when the Pardoner concludes the telling of his tale with the wish that Christ may bestow *His* pardon, a true pardon, upon the company, I think (though the lines admit other interpretations) that we are intended to see him as calling attention to the radical separation which can exist in practice between the spirit and the letter of religious authority. There is clearly a basis in such examples for supposing that Chaucer was in some degree responsive to Wyclif's emphasis, elaborated and often distorted by the Lollard apologists who sought to apply his ideas, on the importance of a Christian's own conscience in determining his spiritual orientation, apart from the sanctions officially offered by the church.

A broader influence on English philosophy in Chaucer's day was the thought of William Ockham. It is an exaggeration to speak of "Ockham's razor" as having severed philosophy from theology, though this is often suggested; but it is true that his denial of the reality of universals (i.e., such general terms as "man") as anything but mental concepts, and of the necessity of secondary causes (since God is equally capable of accomplishing directly anything which He can effect through a secondary cause), and his confinement of *scientia,* or real knowledge, to the sphere of observation and logical inference tended in this direction. They allowed little to be affirmed about the relation of created life to God beyond the acknowledgment through faith of His omnipotence and goodness and the ethical imperative of obeying His commands, and imposed new responsibilities on the sciences, which thus became largely independent of the constraints of theology. Thomas Bradwardine reemphasized the intimate involvement of God with creation, and specifically with human life, in his *De causa Dei* ("On Divine Causation"), written to counter the "Pelagianism" of Ockham and others whom he saw as allowing too great an autonomy to humanity's free will. Though he seems to have taken pains to define a position which would avoid both acquiescence in astrological determinism and an overemphasis on the predetermining influence of God, his thought has been seen as wholly opposed to human freedom in its implications and certainly foreshadows in a number of ways later predestinationist theology. Though Chaucer's Nun's Priest cites Bradwardine, with Augustine and Boethius, as one who has wrestled with the problem of free will, it is by no means clear that this implies an endorsement of his position.

Without positing any direct influence, we may see Chaucer's distancing of himself in the *Canterbury Tales* from the sort of orientation provided by poetic tradition and his reliance on the vivid but often distorted vision of his characters to indicate the relation of spiritual, philosophical, and social values to their lives as his equivalent to the operation of Ockham's razor, reducing religious authority to the rudiments of faith and compelling us to begin on the fundamental level of observation in our evaluation of the pilgrimage. It is true that the antiallegorical aspect of the poetry of Jean de Meun anticipates this tendency in Chaucer and does so largely under the influence of positivist tendencies in the thought of his own day, but Chaucer goes further than Jean in dealing with the problems posed by the denial of universals, a denial whose epistemological consequences may be said to parallel the difficulties posed by the denial to poetry of the implications of order and coherence embodied in allegory. He accepts more completely the conditions such a constraining philosophy imposes, and the counterpart in the *Tales* to his earlier search for the place and value of human love is a varied and complex exploration of the possible sources of meaning in life as lived on the broadest possible plane.

Theseus's evocation of the benevolent "Firste Moevere" amounts to a leap of faith, and a pervasive concern of the *Tales* as a whole is the psychological effect of living in the absence of any more immediate confirmation of order and providence than such a leap provides. Some characters deal with the absence of certainty by refusing to concern themselves with the question, "Who hath the world in honde?"; others reveal their anxiety in such neurotic forms as the Man of Law's vacillating attitude toward providence or the Pardoner's compulsive blasphemy; the Nun's Priest seems to have made spiritual peace with the likelihood that certainty about the large questions of providence and self-determination is unattainable; and perhaps the Clerk, illustrating his Christian and Boethian conviction that God tests but never merely tempts humanity through the scarcely credible humility of Griselda, provides the strongest example of steadfastness.

Chaucer seems finally to share the general lack of certainty of his characters, and though it seems futile to attempt any more precise spiritual or philosophical interpretation of the malaise itself, it is possible to see at least a partial coming to terms with it in Chaucer's handling of the implications of individual character. He places an extraordinary emphasis on the obstacles to vision and knowledge presented by the situations of his characters and goes to exceptional lengths to locate and dramatize their inherent capacities for love and spirituality. In one aspect, the Friar and the Pardoner are common embodiments of religious corruption, but, from another point of view, the knowledge that the Pardoner's alienation and bitterness are partly caused by a congenital sexual deficiency gives us grounds for sympathy which are absent in the Friar's case; we may go further and see in the Pardoner's fascination with hazard and blasphemy, his nervous eloquence and vivid evocation of the *timor mortis,* the perversion of what is basically a deeply religious nature, something we cannot detect in the cold and self-serving eloquence of the Friar. Again, the Wife of Bath, appealing as we are bound to find her, has nonetheless squandered her life and love in a way which makes her for some an allegorical embodiment of spiritual barrenness. But a capacity, at least, for richer moral and spiritual life is revealed by her tale, with its celebration of *gentilesse* and its glimpse of a sexual harmony attained through charity and submissiveness. To compare such characters as the Wife and the Pardoner with the figures of hypocrisy and debauchery in the *Roman de la Rose* on whom they are modeled in many respects is to appreciate the largely redeeming effect of Chaucer's deepening and complicating of their natures and the delicacy with which he insinuates a vestigial idealism into his most powerfully realistic creations. We may also see him asserting a very different view of human freedom from that of Wyclif, with his emphasis on the Christian's obligation of self-determination, or that of Bradwardine, who declared that while the stars may help to determine character, and circumstance may temporarily hinder or confuse one's judgment, only in submission to God is one's basic capacity to will freely governed in any way.

In any evaluation of the characters of the *Canterbury Tales,* it would seem, intuition and sympathy must take priority over theological and moral rigor, and to the intellectual issues raised by their situations Chaucer offers no clear answer. We may conclude by observing that in Chaucer's poetry as a whole the quest for intellectual certainty is presented as one that cannot be achieved on its own terms. The secret of a securely ordered life can be compared to the Philosopher's Stone, with which the Canon's Yeoman points the moral of his tale:

> The philosophres sworn were everychoon
> That they sholden discovere it unto noon,
> Ne in no book it write in no manere.
> For unto Crist it is so lief and deere
> That he wol nat that it discovered bee,
> But where it liketh to his deitee
> Men for t'enspire, . . .   (1464–70)

BIBLIOGRAPHIC NOTE

A number of books and articles deal in more detail with points touched briefly in this essay. On Chaucer's use of poetry as a medium for analyzing intellectual questions and his skepticism about final answers, see Sheila Delany, *Chaucer's House of Fame: The Poetics of Skeptical Fideism* (Chicago: University of Chicago Press, 1972). On his use of medieval science in creating character, see Walter Clyde Curry, *Chaucer and the Mediaeval*

Sciences, 2nd ed. (New York: Barnes & Noble, 1960); and on his use of astrology, see Chauncey Wood, *Chaucer and the Country of the Stars* (Princeton; Princeton University Press, 1970). On the "intellectual tradition" in twelfth- and thirteenth-century poetry, see D. S. Brewer, "The Relationship of Chaucer to the English and Continental Traditions," in *Chaucer and Chaucerians* (University: University of Alabama Press, 1966), pp. 1–38. On the cosmological "model" bequeathed by late antiquity to medieval poets, see C. S. Lewis, *The Discarded Image* (Cambridge; at the University Press, 1964). On *natura* as theme and persona in poetry from the twelfth century to Chaucer, see George Economou, *The Goddess Natura in Medieval Literature* (Cambridge, Mass.: Harvard University Press, 1972). On intellectual elements in medieval love poetry, see Peter Dronke, "L'amor che move il sole e l'altre stelle," *Studi medievali,* 6 (1965), 389–422; *Medieval Latin and the Rise of European Love-Lyric,* 2 vols. (Oxford: at the Clarendon Press, 1965). On the *Roman de la Rose* and philosophical love poetry, see Winthrop Wetherbee, "The Literal and the Allegorical: Jean de Meun and the *De planctu naturae,*" *Medieval Studies,* 33 (1971), 264–91. On religious issues in Chaucer's day, see W. A. Pantin, *The English Church in the Fourteenth Century* (Cambridge; at the University Press, 1955); and Herbert B. Workman, *John Wyclif, a Study of the English Medieval Church,* 2 vols., (Oxford: at the Clarendon Press, 1926). On the impact of Ockham and fourteenth-century reactions, see Arthur Stephen McGrade, *The Political Thought of William of Ockham: Personal and Institutional Principles* (Cambridge: at the University Press, 1974); and Heiko A. Oberman, *Archbishop Thomas Bradwardine, A Fourteenth-Century Augustinian* (Utrecht: Kemink, 1957). The most useful English translation and edition of Boethius's *The Consolation of Philosophy* is by Richard Green (Indianapolis and New York: Bobbs-Merrill, 1962).

Hope Phyllis Weissman

Antifeminism and Chaucer's Characterization of Women

Antifeminism in literary tradition, defined strictly, refers to those writings which revenge themselves upon woman's failure to conform to male specifications by presenting her as a nagging bully and an avaricious whore. Though the attitude arose in part from certain premises of classical and Judeo-Christian philosophies, by the later Middle Ages it had developed into a tradition of social and personal satire, providing rich opportunities for the deployment of a caricature sometimes mischievous but often sour. Chaucer was the heir and the most versatile manipulator of this literary tradition which, on his knees before Queen Alceste in the literary meadow of the *Legend of Good Women,* he comically—and disingenuously—disavowed.[1]

[1] A medieval scholar's bibliography of antifeminist literature is supplied by the Wife of Bath's citation of her husband Jankyn's "book of wikked wyves" (*WB Prol,* 669–81). Its contents include: Theophrastus, *The Golden Book of Marriage,* 3rd century B.C.; Saint Jerome, *Against Jovinian,* 393 A.D.; and Walter Map, *Dissuasion of Valerius from Taking a Wife,* c. 1200. To these works in Latin should certainly be added two in French: Jean de Meun's portion of *The Romance of the Rose,* c. 1275, and Eustache Deschamp's *Mirror of Marriage,* c. 1385. A lengthy bibliography of medieval and Tudor antifeminist writings in English is assembled by Francis Lee Utley, *The Crooked Rib* (Columbus, Ohio: Ohio State University Press, 1944). But for an important investigation of "feminist" tendencies in the writings of the Church Fathers which places the antifeminist tradition in a new perspective, see JoAnn McNamara, "Sexual Equality and the Cult of Virginity in Early Christian Thought," Papers of the Berkshire Conference on the History of Women, II (Radcliffe College, 1974).

The literary tradition of antifeminism may, however, be defined in a wider sense to include not simply satirical caricatures of women but any presentation of a woman's nature intended to conform her to male expectations of what she is or ought to be, not her own. By this wider definition, an image of woman need not be ostensibly unflattering to be antifeminist in fact or in potential; indeed, the most insidious of antifeminist images are those which celebrate, with a precision often subtle rather than apparent, the forms a woman's goodness is to take. Chaucer recognized this wider definition of antifeminism too. Writing the *Canterbury Tales,* as he did, to investigate the capacity of received forms of human experience to embody adequately the experience of late medieval man, it is hardly surprising that received forms of woman's experience should come under his close scrutiny.

In accordance with this wider definition of antifeminism, our purpose in the following pages will be twofold: first, briefly to trace the development and indicate the antifeminist implications of the established medieval images of women which continued to exert compelling force on the minds and actions of Chaucer's contemporaries; and second, more extensively to examine the different ways Chaucer himself investigates the implications of the established images and their impress on the human spirit in his *Canterbury Tales*.

Medieval culture by Chaucer's time had distinguished four images of women as primary, primary in the sense that the alternative conceptions of women they defined provided the basic vocabulary of individual character creation. Of these four images, two were secular and two were religious; and to paraphrase the Wife of Bath's assessment of her husbands, two of them were good and two were bad. The "good" and "bad" (ostensibly flattering and unflattering) images of the religious tradition had their origin in the female characterizations of Scriptural narrative as apprehended through the Pauline conception of the Old and the New Man (see I Corinthians 15). The Old Testament Woman, Eve the mate of Adam, like him was bound by the laws of the flesh and the material universe; conversely, the New Testament Woman, Virgin Mary the mother of Christ, was freed by the law of grace to enjoy the pleasures of the spiritual realm.

It took very little "glosynge" of the Creation and Fall myth of Genesis 2–3 to extract the Parson's antifeminist moral lesson that God created Eve to be Adam's servant and so that, when she seizes the mastery, the world is turned "up-so-doun." Eve's gluttonous behavior in the Garden defines her as being the essence of carnality; yet, in addition, her lust for material and intellectual possession is a deliberate act of rebellion against the Maker who created her to be second-rate. In this rebellion against the limitations of her created image, Eve is, we shall see, the direct model for Chaucer's new fleshly protestant, the Wife of Bath.

The medieval Church's conception of the New Woman as an antithesis and a corrective to the Old found its principal literary model in the Infancy Narrative of Luke's Gospel. The antiphonal narrative structure of the Infancy uses Elizabeth's conception of John the Baptist to recreate the Old Testament ethos and highlight its revolutionary ethical theme. Thus whereas Elizabeth, like Sarah and Hannah, considers her barrenness reproachful, Mary learns that perpetual virginity will be the reason for her exaltation. Where Elizabeth's renewed capacity leads to a public celebration, Mary conceives in tranquility and stores God's favor in her heart. And where Elizabeth's husband Zachariah questions God's ordinance, the Virgin Mary, correcting Eve as well as the Old Testament priesthood, obediently kneels in assent. In the later Middle Ages, this obedient kneeling was to become increasingly conspicuous until, with Virginia of the *Physician's Tale,* it suffered a pratfall. By this did the Roman maiden acknowledge her model's compelling power.

The Old Eve and New Mary images of women in religious tradition had their counterparts in the two principal secular literary traditions, the courtly and the bourgeois. The bourgeois image of woman, represented most clearly in the Old French fabliaux, inherits directly from Eve her lust for material possession which, in the marketplace mentality of medieval town and village, becomes a gathering of sex and coin. The fabliau woman gathers these possessions from within but primarily from outside the marriage bond; she ventures outside not simply because her husband is inadequate, though he is often so, but more significantly because her lust of possession is insatiable—and is matched by a correspondingly inexhaustible supply of physical energy and mental craft. There is no evidence, for example, that the merchant husband of the *Shipman's Tale* is either physically unsatisfactory or niggardly; his dame is simply playing the Eve game of testing how much is too much.

Although the origin of the courtly image of woman remains a

controversial subject, one important source of the conception, surely, was the worship of the Great Mother goddesses in the cults of pagan antiquity. Indeed, the Early Church was responding directly to these cults when it elevated the Virgin to her seat beside God's throne after the Assumption; from there she reigned as the Mother of an imperfect humanity, the source of its wisdom and love. The courtly image of woman conveyed in the Provençal and Italian stilnovist lyric of the High Middle Ages is as clearly a counterpart of this cult image of the Virgin as it is a parody of the feudal lord. The lyricist's *dompna,* physically chaste if not perfect, is exalted like the Virgin herself because of her spiritual superiority; and her function, similarly, is to allure from her pedestal and lead men to wisdom through love. Whatever Eleanor of Aquitaine and her daughters may have intended by encouraging the celebration of the courtly lady, therefore, the image came to function, as did that of the Virgin, for the benefit of their celebrating men.[2]

Perhaps still more important to the courtly conception of woman in the later Middle Ages is an aspect of the image we may designate the Courtly Damsel. The Damsel is distinguishable from the Lady by a significant shift in emphasis: if the Lady drew men to her tower because of her transcending virtue, the Damsel attracts them by her sympathetic weakness; she is not the star but the trophy who, in the popular romances, was bestowed upon her dragon-slaying men. Like the image of the Courtly Lady proper, the image of the Damsel is paralleled by the image of the helpless Virgin in later medieval devotional art; like the Lady, too, the Damsel is traceable ultimately to conceptions of women in pagan antiquity. Although the Damsel is most frequently seen as a descendent of the helpless-young-thing heroines of the Greek romances, in fact the *locus classicus* of the conception for medieval secular literature was the treatment of Lavinia in Virgil's *Aëneid.*

Virgil's conception of Lavinia may be considered a radicalization of Homer's conception of Briseis, in the *Iliad,* as a pawn in a man's world. Although the importance of Lavinia as bride of Rome's founder is suggested in *Aeneid* Two and established clearly in Seven, it is not until the epic's conclusion that she

---

[2]The most comprehensive treatment of the medieval Marian tradition available in English remains Yrjö Hirn's *The Sacred Shrine* (London: Macmillan, 1912), Part II. For the ethical significance of the feminine image in the courtly love system, see Frederick Goldin, *The Mirror of Narcissus* (Ithaca, N.Y.: Cornell University Press, 1967).

directly motivates the conflict between Aeneas and Turnus. More significant still, Lavinia motivates the conflict by inadvertence. Her mother Amata, endeavoring to persuade Turnus not to enter a duel with Aeneas, has threatened that if her young hero should die, she will die also. Hearing this, Lavinia's

> hot cheeks were bathed in tears; . . .
> and her blush, a kindled fire, crossed
> her burning face. And just as when a craftsman
> stains Indian ivory with blood-red purple,
> or when white lilies, mixed with many roses,
> blush: even such, the colors of the virgin.
> His love drives Turnus wild; he stares at his
> Lavinia; even keener now for battle[3]

The lilies mixed with roses, the mingled blushes and tears, above all the inciting power of uncomprehendingly innocent beauty—all these features, in the medieval centuries, become part of the Damsel canon. They are recapitulated almost exactly in the figure of Emily, heroine of the *Knight's Tale*, but with the significant difference that Emily momentarily comprehends, and too well.

For his first Canterbury tale, Chaucer transformed Boccaccio's classicizing romance *Il Teseida* into a sympathetically critical examination of the chivalric life in its aspects of lovemaking and statecraft. It is a man's world his Knight-narrator has made, centering on the courtly love posturings of Arcite and Palamon and, more particularly, the rulership of Theseus; the women of the tale, Hippolyta and Emily, are essentially aspects of the concerns of their men. The Knight's characterizations of the heroines present them as having been mastered at the outset, in this feature contrasting significantly with Boccaccio's, which appear to assert their independence before the author closes in. Boccaccio's Hippolyta, in *Teseida* One, performs the antique virago with spirit, though the romance proceeds to ignore her once she is subjugated by the Athenian men. Boccaccio's Emilia, in *Teseida* Three, operates freely within courtly romance conventions—but this representation soon proves to be the booby trap of a lover's wrath.

[3]*The Aeneid of Virgil,* Allen Mandelbaum, trans. (New York: Bantam Books, 1972), Book XII, 11.89–96.

The freedom of Boccaccio's Emilia first suggests itself rhetorically when the heroine is ushered in by a catalog of spring's perfections yet, though she weaves the season's roses with her charmingly white hands, is not required to submit her own perfections to the expected catalog enumeration. The rhetorical freedom immediately acquires a psychological dimension when we hear that "beautiful young Emilia, as dawn broke each morning, entered alone into the garden which opened out from her room, drawn there by her own nature, not because she was bound by love" (Canto 8).[4] When the heroine is seen by the two young heroes, her freedom becomes the basis of a thematic contrast; their vision of her from their palace prison instantly subjects them to love bondage while Emilia, overhearing their sighs, plays on with a new toy: "As it seemed to her that she knew that she was indeed liked, she took pleasure in it, and considered herself more beautiful, and now adorned herself the more every time she returned to the garden" (Canto 19). But finally the playful freedom of Emilia becomes the occasion of her author's jealousy as Boccaccio vents his masculine resentment on the tease he has created her to be: "Almost stripped of any other worth, they [women] are satisfied to be praised for beauty, and by contriving to please by their charm, they enslave others while they keep themselves free" (Canto 30).

Chaucer's characterization of Emily implies that he perfectly recognized this authorial self-deception, for the Knight's heroine pretends to no freedom of either rhetorical or psychological design. Rhetorically, the Knight interweaves the formal description of the season and the description of the heroine's person so that, as in contemporary tapestries, she becomes part of patterned Nature itself.[5] Familiar images of the lily and the rose define at once the beauties of May and the beauties of its finest flower:

> Til it fil ones, in a morwe of May,
> That Emelye, that fairer was to sene
> Than is the lylie upon his stalke grene,
> And fressher than the May with floures newe—
> For with the rose colour stroof hire hewe,   (1034–38)

[4]Citations of Boccaccio are from *The Book of Theseus*, Bernadette Marie McCoy, trans. (New York: Medieval Text Association, 1974). The authoritative edition of the Italian is *Giovanni Boccaccio: Teseida*, S. Battaglia, ed. (Florence: Accademia della Crusca, 1938).

[5]For the rhetorical background as well as a discussion of the Emily portrait, see D. S. Brewer, "The Ideal of Feminine Beauty in Medieval Literature," *Modern Language Review*, 50 (1955), 257–69.

Not only the details of Emily's physical appearance but also her actions, in the Knight's treatment, become part of the seasonal patterning. In contrast to the playful and largely undirected activity of Boccaccio's Emilia, the Knight's arises on a special morning, a holiday, at the direct command of the personified season to "do thyn observaunce" (1045). The careful regularization of the poet's language incorporates the heroine's movements into the seasonal ritual:

> And in the gardyn, at the sonne upriste,
> She walketh up and doun, and as her liste
> She gadereth floures, party white and rede,
> To make a subtil gerland for hire hede;
> And as an aungel hevenysshly she soong.   (1051–55)

Admirers of the Knight's portrait of Emily surely are correct in recognizing its superiority to the usual description of the courtly damsel; no mere portrait, indeed, it is in fact an emblematic realization of the central impulse of the courtly life, to transmute nature into a work of art. Within the portrait this impulse is represented symbolically by a detail not so treated in Boccaccio, Emily's "yelow heer . . . broyded in a tresse/ Bihynde her bak, a yerde long, I gesse" (1049–50). From this perception that Emily's portrait is an emblem of the courtly life, however, it follows that the portrait does not function as in Boccaccio to introduce the story's heroine. It serves rather as the object of aristocratic contemplation and, more specifically, as the starting point of an action which physically and psychically concerns the male. The Knight's Emily, in contrast to Boccaccio's, is not simply appealingly unselfconscious in her garden scene; like Lavinia, she is virtually without psychological dimension. Whereas Boccaccio's Emilia was able to overhear the young men's love agonies and used the knowledge as a basis for her own maneuverings, the Knight's heroine—whose portrait is isolated rhetorically from the love-plot action by the ironic framing images of the young men in the prison tower (1030–32, 1056–61)—remains oblivious of the kind of attention her image has elicited.

After Emily's image has been implanted in the lovers' minds, moreover, their love agonies and feud develop, again as with Lavinia, in complete independence of her presence and control. The independence, indeed, reaches a point of virtual absurdity when Arcite and Palamon engage in a duel to the death over the image, years later, without ever having once tested its reality. Theseus, coming upon the lovers in the forest, takes the Olympian view that it is "yet the beste game of alle" (1806) that Emily "woot namoore of al this hoote fare,/ By God, than woot a cok-kow or an hare!" (1809–10). The Olympian view means, how-ever, that the Duke's lordly recognition of Emily's predicament by no means entails his interest in resolving it for the sake of a mere cuckoo. Instead of deferring to the decision of the heroine herself, as does Dame Nature in the not dissimilar circumstances of the *Parliament of Fowls,* Theseus, rather, tacitly accepts the premise of the heroes' combat and simply elevates that combat into a public tournament—transforming personal male emotional activity into a public ritual of the male state.

Nothing in the Knight-narrator's account of Theseus's deci-sion suggests his awareness of its ungenerosity to the heroine, but Chaucer's own unease about the decision and its premises is implied in his treatment of Emily in the one scene which repre-sents the *Knight's Tale* heroine as a psychological being. The scene, which takes place in the temple of Diana on the morning before the tournament, shows Emily again performing ritual observances—and praying for deliverance from men. This is cer-tainly not the tenor of the prayer spun out by Boccaccio's heroine in *Teseida* Seven, however much the mere content of the two prayers may seem to run parallel. For what Boccaccio's Emilia finally requests of the hunting goddess—after due acknowledg-ment of her militant chastity and Emilia's own previous dedica-tion to it (Cantos 79–82)—is help in choosing between two equally appealing young men: "if the Fates have decreed that I be sub-jected to the law of Juno, you must certainly forgive me for it" (Canto 83) and "grant that the one who loves me more, the one who desires me with greater constancy may come to my arms, for I myself do not know which one to choose, so winsome does each one seem to me" (Canto 85).

The sophisticated familiarity with which Boccaccio's Emilia addresses Diana becomes, in the prayer of the Knight's heroine, an expression of personal terror. Emily's terror, specifically her fear of violation, is presented as an all-pervading anxiety which even colors her perception of the very goddess whose protection she implores: "As keepe me fro thy vengeaunce and thyn ire,/ That Attheon aboughte cruelly" (2302–3). The direct source of her anxiety, however, is clearly her perception of the loss of freedom and identity, the exploitation, which in her view the relationship with a man necessarily entails. It is thus the Knight's Emily, not Boccaccio's, who prays unequivocally to remain forever a maid,

> And for to walken in the wodes wilde,
> And noght to ben a wyf and be with childe,
> Noght wol I knowe the compaignye of man.   (2309–11)

and who concludes her prayer by imploring the virgin goddess with whom she identifies to insulate her permanently from the exigencies of the courting life (2328–30).

Emily's prayer of course is not granted; the courting life requires her complete subjugation and requires not only the relinquishing of her body but the elimination of her independent will. In this context, Boccaccio's antifeminist diatribe against Emilia's prompt inclination toward the victorious Arcite (*Teseida* Eight, 124–28) takes on a new aspect:

> And she agayn hym caste a freendlich ye
> (For wommen, as to speken in comune,
> Thei folwen alle the favour of Fortune)
> And was al his chiere, as in his herte.   (2680–83)

The Knight's Emily has become an automaton: she falls in love to order just as she swoons to order in mourning Arcite (2817–26) and just as she marries Palamon to order in the tale's conclusion, when Theseus presses the courtly image of woman into the service of a state affair:

> Lene me youre hond, for this is oure accord.
> Lat se now of youre wommanly pitee.
> He is a kynges brother sone, pardee;   (3082–84)

Emily's final fate in the *Knight's Tale* thus is to become a work of the art of diplomacy: it is not a Galatea but a scroll of parchment that the chivalric mind has wrought.

When Chaucer arranged for the Miller to "quyt" the Knight's sympathetic critique of the chivalric life with an equally sympathetic critique of the bourgeois, he provided also that an examination of the fabliau image of woman would be a central part of the criticism. In this as in other respects, the method of the Miller's tale is to literalize and caricature features of the Knight's; thus, his heroine Alison, like Emily, is a prisoner of male expectations, but the contours of her prison have become the parlor of a burgher Annunciation and the vat of "Nowelis" flood.[6] Unlike

---

[6]The biblical parodies are discussed in their relation to medieval drama by Beryl B. Rowland, "The Play of the *Miller's Tale*: A Game within a Game," *The Chaucer Review*, 5 (1970), 140–46.

her courtly counterpart, Alison at the beginning of the *Miller's Tale* has already passed under the yoke of marriage. Her *mésalliance* with the "riche gnof" John the Carpenter, in an exuberant parody of the Mary-Joseph domestic situation, quickly admits her to the prison of her husband's bedroom and mind:

> Jalous he was, and heeld her narwe in cage,
> For she was wylde and yong, and he was old,
> And demed hymself been lik a cokewold.   (3224–26)

Within her physical "cage," Alison, more like Boccaccio's than the Knight's heroine, proves adept at satisfying her sexual desires and, beyond them, her need for amusement.[7] Yet if her physical gratification with "hende" Nicholas has a natural vitality which exempts it from criticism, the mental titillation achieved by exploiting "joly" Absolon literally reduces her to an ass. This seamy episode, together with the unmistakable cruelty of John's treatment in the tale's apocalyptic conclusion, requires one to recognize that Alison's "free play" within her physical prison is ultimately insignificant; she will never be released from compulsorily fulfilling the expectations of her husband's fabliau mind.

Alison's final imprisonment in the fabliau image is effectively predicted at her introduction when the Miller ushers in his heroine through a parody of the rhetorical *descriptio* of the romance lady (3233–70). It is sometimes urged that Alison's portrait is a triumphant celebration of late medieval naturalism, but a closer inspection of the natural images reveals that few of them are innocent of innuendo. Even the most wholesome, "as whit as morne milk" (3236), does not grace this dairymaid's neck but rather the "barmclooth" covering her loins. The suggestion is subtly reinforced when her breath is compared to a "hoord of apples leyd in hey or heeth" (3262) and finally trumpeted, for all its tactful line-ordering, by the portrait's sublimely bathetic conclusion:

> She was a prymerole, a piggesnye,
> For any lord to leggen in his bedde,
> Or yet for any good yeman to wedde.   (3268–70)

---

[7]For the Boethian source of the cage image and its implications, see George Economou, "Chaucer's Use of the Boethian Bird in the Cage Image in the *Canterbury Tales*," forthcoming in *Philological Quarterly*.

The Miller's Alison, as a caricature of the Courtly Damsel, is not an earth mother but a sex object; and as a caricature of the courtly art of grace, she is a "wezele" (3234) full of craft. The Knight would have us believe that Emily's art, like Perdita's in *The Winter's Tale*, "is an art/ That nature makes" (IV, iv, 91–92), since the only sign of her own contriving is the long gold braid at her back. The gossiping Miller's jovial reply is that Alison acts as her own *Natura,* plucking her perfect brows (3245) and running silk braids around her purse (3250–51). Naturally her highly scrubbed forehead shines like a gold noble, perhaps reflecting the brooch on her collar which, "as brood as is the boos of a bokeler" (3266), marks the order of Alison of Bath. For all the physicality of young Alison's portrait, considerable attention is thus lavished on ornament and, notably in the morning-milk image, on ornamented clothes. Alison's body is overlaid with white cloth and outlined by blackthread embroidery; a girdle bars her waist, laces crosshatch her legs—if this heroine indeed must resemble a barn fowl, the barn fowl is etched in grisaille. Grisaille windows became increasingly fashionable in English churches after the mid-fourteenth century, and in a smallish town like Oxford they might still have appeared newfangled. Set against the grisaille Alison, the Knight's Emily—all green and gold, parti-white and red—presents an image not at all in living color but cut from an earlier mold.

Chaucer's characterizations of Emily and Alison, though offered in the first two Canterbury tales, may be accepted nevertheless as his definitive statements on the courtly and bourgeois images of women. Later tales attempt to match these portraits only under special circumstances; the more interesting are those which show Chaucer extending the techniques of the early characterizations to explore other traditional images of women or indeed to invent new combinations of traditional images. Thus when Chaucer extends the technique of the *Knight's Tale* to the Clerk's tale of patient Griselda, he not only intensifies the saint's legend genre by importing material from the Marian apocrypha. He also intensifies the heroine's cryptic protests against the suffrance required by her holy image by adding critical apostrophes in the narrator's own voice. And when Chaucer reuses the parodic technique of the *Miller's Tale* in the Merchant's tale of May and January, he contrives that the heroine's deflation from courtly into bourgeois image will be recapitulated through religious images in the tale's brilliant finale. With January's paradisal garden as her setting, May becomes a caricature of the Virgin Bride in the allegorized Canticles; yet when she climbs into an Augustinian pear tree and the arms of her serpent-lover Damian, after all she fulfills the "plit" of mortal women (2335) to suffer the soiled nature of Eve.[8]

The most significant invention in Chaucer's Canterbury characterizations of women, however, transcends technique altogether because it issues directly from his decision of the mid-1380s to redefine the essence of his art. In his characterizations of the Prioress and the Wife of Bath, both in their *General Prologue* portraits and in their tales, Chaucer confronts his audience with the New and Old Women in the form of living images. His purpose is to focus attention on the difficulty of self-realization in an environment which presses such images on human beings.

The Prioress of the *General Prologue* believes herself to be cooperating with her environment by conforming herself to the New Woman image; she conforms to the wrong one. Studying, with the aid of the *Roman de la Rose,* how to play the courtly lady (127ff.), Madame Eglantyne has not simply denied the nun's vocation, she has also denied herself. As Chaucer the Pilgrim inadvertently tells us, the Prioress's human nature is too big to be forced into images, "for, hardily, she was nat undergrowe" (156). This vision of the Prioress's self-constriction is heightened in her tale's invocation where, her study now the Virgin's humility, she grovels in the role of a suckling child (1674). The barely suppressed natural energies of the Prioress, finding no other outlet, channel themselves into her characterization of her Virginal exemplar: the Virgin of the invocation, whose purity "ravyshedest doun" the Holy Spirit (1659–60); the Virgin of the miracle story, whose motherly love permanently infantilizes her men. The Prioress thus realizes the New Woman image with a vengeance; but the great avenger, so she would have us believe, is that Old Woman par excellence, the Wife of Bath.

The Wife's characterization is presented in three parts—her *General Prologue* portrait, the self-portrait in her own prologue, and the hag-princess of her fairy tale—in which a special kind of progression may be detected. The sequence moves from a com-

---

[8]On Chaucer's use of biblical and apocryphal materials, see further F. L. Utley, "Five Genres in the *Clerk's Tale,*" *The Chaucer Review,* 6 (1971–72), 198–228; and Emerson Brown, "Biblical Women in *The Merchant's Tale:* Feminism, Antifeminism, and Beyond," *Viator,* 5 (1974), 387–412.

paratively straightforward confirmation of the Old Woman image in its most negative valuation, through a massive display of propaganda which strategically manipulates the negative image while arguing a newly positive evaluation of it, to climax in an attempted rejection of the Old Woman image whether positively or negatively regarded. The Wife of Bath is most truly the feminist in her effort to dispense with images of women altogether, but the Wife of Bath is also imprisoned by the antifeminism of her culture, for in her tale's conclusion the image becomes her will.

Chaucer the Pilgrim's portrait of the "good Wif . . . of biside Bathe" (445), in this interpretation, functions primarily to establish the image of the Wife as an incarnation of the fabliau woman and more especially the Old Eve. With a characteristically late medieval richness of determination, Chaucer summons the materials of both experience and authority to supply the concrete details of the portrait. Thus, the apparently naturalistic detail of the Wife's gap-tooth (468) is lifted from physiognomy manuals to serve as an emblem of her lusty vagrancy; similarly, the documentary-seeming vignette of her social competition during the Church offering (449–52) descends from traditional satire on the prideful womanly estate. Two further details of the Wife's portrait, however, the picture of the Wife as mock-knight (469–73) and the precise localization of her cloth making (445, 447–48), point beyond particular sources to the primary source of the portrait as a whole. Chaucer has conceived the Wife of Bath's portrait not simply as a creative agglomeration of features deriving from Alison and Eve but rather as a very nearly systematic parody of one very popular positive conception of the Old Testament Woman. The portrait is in fact a parody of the Virtuous Woman (*mulier fortis*) of Proverbs 31, who, in the tradition of scriptural exegesis established by the Fathers, was regarded as a figure of the Church and of the New Woman Mary in her most militant aspect.[9]

The picture of the Wife as mock-knight—with hat "brood as is a bokeler or a targe," footmantle around her hips, sharp spurs (470–73)—thus may be recognized as a comic literalization of the proverbial "she girdeth her loins with strength, and strengtheneth her arms. . . . Strength and honor are her clothing" (31:17,25). And equally the Wife's prominent position in the late-

[9]Some important references: Augustine, *Sermo 37,* in *Patrologia Latina* **38,** cols. 221–35; Bede, "De muliere forti," in *PL* 91, cols. 1039–52; and Bernard, *Super missus est homilia* 2:5, 11, in *PL* 183, cols. 63, 66.

fourteenth-century clothing industry—"Of clooth-makyng she hadde swich an haunt,/ She passed hem of Ypres and of Gaunt" (447–48)—may be understood as a quite literal capitalization on the Virtuous Woman's traditional office: "She layeth her hands to the spindle, and her hands hold the distaff. . . . She maketh fine linen, and selleth it; and delivereth girdles unto the merchant" (31:19,24). But it is surely the Wife's extension of her capitalist mentality into the marriage industry that provides the most devastating comment on her "realization" of the Virtuous Woman image. The Woman of Proverbs, fruitful not only of goods but of services, is "prized above rubies" (31:10) because "the heart of her husband doth safely trust in her. . . . She will do him good and not evil all the days of her life. . . . Her husband is known in the gates, when he sitteth among the elders of the land" (31:11,12,23). The Wife of Bath's parade of husbands, on the other hand, must have been notorious at the "gates"; she too

> was a worthy womman al hir lyve:
> Housbondes at chirche dore she hadde fyve,
> Withouten oother compaignye in youth . . .
>
> *(Gen Prol,* 459–61)[10]

Alison of Bath's quantification of good wifehood in her successive marriage ceremonies does indeed become the central issue in the self-portraying prologue which precedes her tale.[11] This prologue is full of surprises, reflecting some of the most significant decisions of Chaucer's artistic career, not the least of which is the opening statement, which represents the archwife in a posture of humble submission to the antifeminist clerks:

> Experience, though noon auctoritee
> Were in this world, is right ynogh for me
> To speke of wo that is in mariage . . .   (1–3)

[10]Additional parallels in the portrait: the Wife's "coverchiefs" (453) caricature Proverbs 31:22, her "wandrynge by the weye" (467) misdirects Proverbs 31:27; her five pilgrimages literalize Proverbs 31:14; and, for that matter, her prominence at the church offering (449–50) is a pushy version of Proverbs 31:20, 29.

[11]Since there are as many interpretations of the *Wife of Bath's Prologue* and *Tale* as there are Chaucer critics, I merely cite three recent analyses which seem to me particularly stimulating even when I do not agree: Norman N. Holland, "Meaning as Transformation: *The Wife of Bath's Tale,*" *College English,* 28 (1967), 279–90; David S. Reid, "Crocodilian Humor: A Discussion of Chaucer's Wife of Bath," *The Chaucer Review,* 4 (1969–70), 73–89; and Beryl Rowland, "Chaucer's Dame Alys: Critics in Blunderland?" *Neuphilologische Mitteilungen,* 73 (1972), 381–95.

Unexpectedly, the Wife promises to duplicate the Old Woman image of the *General Prologue* portrait, using her sexual experience to confirm the assertion of celibate authority that marriage equals torture by one's wife. Expectedly, she very quickly wanders from her stated promise, like Eve questioning the limitations imposed on her freedom of movement and mind: "But that I axe, why that the fifthe man/ Was noon housbonde to the Samaritan?" (21–22). Yet unexpectedly again, the Wife's elaborate apology for sexuality, drawing on a rich store of arguments from Scripture and natural philosophy, deliberately caricatures these arguments so that her ostensible defense of appetite becomes an actual self-indictment. Her central text from Scripture, the Old Testament command from Genesis 1:28 that "God bad us for to wexe and multiplye" (28) the world's population, thus quickly becomes an authorization to increase her own store of bedmates (30–34). New Testament prescriptions for marital conduct, especially the Pauline instructions of I Corinthians 7, are wrested out of context similarly to license deploying her "instrument/ As frely as my Makere hath it sent" (149–50) while converting each husband into a "dettour and . . . thral" (155) to one devouring queen bee.

The perversity of the Wife's self-justification usually is read as an artist's joke on both the woman and her detractors; in fact it represents Chaucer's profound and sympathetic insight into the effects of antifeminism on the feminine nature. Chaucer here recognizes that the antifeminist image of Old Eve, a product of the mentality which regards natural appetite as unnatural, by compelling the Wife merely to quantify sexuality has thereby ensured her sterility. He sees that she can have nothing to gain from a defense of sexuality which celebrates its fruitfulness, since there can be no display of children to confirm her fulfillment of the "gentil text." And he therefore arranges for the Wife to triumph in this moment of necessity by turning the sterilizing image itself into an asset—for, by flaunting the image of sexual promiscuity, she "covers" the barrenness which is her reproach. The triumph, significantly, is recognized and celebrated by the eunuch Pardoner, who caricatures physical potency to mask the spiritual impotence he suffers within: " 'Now dame,' quod he, 'by God and by seint John!/ Ye been a noble prechour in this cas' " (*WB, Prol,* 164–65). The great difference between the Wife and the Pardoner, certainly, is that the Wife has refused to accept spiritual sterility as her final suffering; the story of her fifth marriage informs us, on the contrary, that in late middle age she has enlisted her deepest resources in a search for creative love. The search, as Chaucer has profoundly understood, must take the form of a direct confrontation with the antifeminist clergy who created the Wife to be grotesque.

The dream which the Wife uses to win the hand of the young clerk Jankyn indicates that she anticipates the usual violation of her nature from this discordant union of Venus and Mercury, but it also suggests that she seeks to make pain its own charm:

> And eek I seyde I mette of hym al nyght,
> He wolde han slayn me as I lay upright,
> And al my bed was ful of verray blood;
> But yet I hope that he shal do me good,
> For blood bitokeneth gold, as me was taught.   (577–81)

The narrative structure of the fifth marriage account precisely fulfills this expectation. The "slaying" is first effected psychologically by Jankyn's sadistic reading of his golden treasury of antifeminism "for his desport" (670) and her torment. The psychological violation becomes physical when the Wife, to silence this aural rape, slaps his cheek and is boxed on the ear. The moment when the Wife lies on the floor "as I were deed" (796) is the moment of blood in her marriage to antifeminism; and it is one which enables the realization of the gold she has dreamed. In another triumph fabricated of necessity, the Wife exploits her vulnerability by assuming the role of martyr in charity (802), thereby manipulating her husband into the corresponding role of guilty sinner who, wholly at her mercy (807), makes complete restitution for his deed: "He yaf me al the bridel in myn hond,/ To han the governance of hous and lond" (813–14). The account makes plain that the redefinition of the marital relationship in which the Wife was both "kynde" and "also trewe, and so was he to me" (823–25) is consequent on her having mastered not only body and property but something far more important. The most precious gold bought by the Wife's blood is the control of her identity, for she also "made him brenne his book anon right tho" (816).

Since the Wife presents her reconciliation with the antifeminists as autobiography, it cannot easily be dismissed as sheer wish fulfillment. Yet Chaucer's use of the "glosynge" Friar to comment on the Wife's discourse at this point (830–31) alerts one to the limitations of the reconciliation. By perpetuating the vocabulary of mastery in marriage, the Wife has failed to articulate the dynamics which move the clerk from complete surrender to the female into a state of mutuality; and she has failed, significantly, to deal directly with the absence of charity which has perverted the nature of her life.

The problem of uncharity is recognized explicitly, if it is not resolved, in the Wife of Bath's fairy tale of the old hag and the young knight. In this third and fullest exploration of the narrative pattern of rape, woman's mastery, and reconciliation, the physical violation—the "lusty bacheler's" rape of the maiden—comes first and is easily dealt with by placing the knight at the mercy of Arthur's queen. The psychological violation which follows—the knight's rejection of the "olde wyf" on their marriage bed—is confronted by the victim herself with the weapon of persuasive rhetoric, a woman's last recourse. The persuasion is embodied in the old wife's bedside lecture on "gentilesse" (1109ff.) which, with the aid of arguments from Boethius, Jean de Meun, and Dante, argues for an appreciation of one human being by another based on inner qualities, not external worth. In context, the old wife's argument emerges as an assertion of the freedom of self-definition—freedom from all established categories or traditionally imposed criteria such as birth, wealth, and beauty—freedom to be, in the fullest Chaucerian sense, "good":

> And therefore, leeve housbonde, I thus conclude:
> Al were it that myne auncestres were rude,
> Yet may the hye God, and so hope I,
> Grante me grace to lyven vertuously. (1171–74)

The old wife's ancestors—perhaps, that is, the antifeminist images of Old Eve which have shadowed her identity—indeed have been "rude," and it may seem that the wife's prayer for grace to live well is answered symbolically in the tale's conclusion by her transformation into a fairy princess, young and fair and good. The major difficulty with such a reading, however, is that the old wife herself does not suggest that her attributes are symbolic but in fact distinctly insists on the reverse. At the conclusion of her lecture, the old wife turns to her silenced partner and in effect dismisses its special message: "But natheless, syn I knowe youre delit,/ I shal fulfille youre worldly appetit" (1217–18). This promise of imminent gratification becomes the young knight's signal; the moral conundrum which she now presents to him he refers back to her with perfect security, for his gesture of submissiveness is actually the psychological trap which the lonely old wife has prepared for her fall. The knight's guise of relinquishing the mastery springs the mechanism which maneuvers the wife into using her powers of self-determination against herself. Willingly she uses them to transform into the courtly damsel men most desire—and women only because they most desire men's love. The conclusion of the *Wife of Bath's Tale* reveals the Wife once again undervaluing the "self-justifying" potential of her material. No mere perversity in this instance, yet far from a triumph in necessity, this conclusion is one of the most deeply pathetic moments in Chaucer's poetry: for the Wife, in struggling to free herself from imprisoning images, has merely transferred her cell.[12]

[12]It has not been possible within the space of this chapter to place Chaucer's characterizations in a broader context of medieval attitudes toward women, but for recent work on the subject, see the papers on "Marriage in the Middle Ages," John Leyerle, ed., *Viator,* 4 (1973), 413–501.

Elizabeth D. Kirk

Chaucer and His English Contemporaries

By one of the paradoxes of literary history, Chaucer's relationship with the bad art of his age is obvious and extremely
illuminating, whereas the better the work of his contemporaries,
the less direct connection with him is perceptible. Even the *Confessio Amantis,* the major English work of his friend John Gower,
becomes less and less like the *Troilus* or the *Canterbury Tales*
the more observantly we read it, so that we can no longer really
understand, except by a tour de force of the historical imagination, how the two poets could have seemed so alike to readers as
late as the Renaissance. Still further removed from Chaucer by
verse form, style, vocabulary, and dialect are his greatest contemporaries, William Langland and the *Pearl*-poet, whose work
though ultimately the most illuminating of all, seem to belong to
another world. These poems were written in the native, ultimately Germanic tradition of alliterative poetry that Chaucer
makes his Parson call so unenthusiastically composition "rum,
ram, ruf, by lettre," and, for any direct evidence we have to the
contrary, Chaucer did not even know them.

Yet, like Shakespeare, Chaucer is best appreciated when we
see him as not only "for all time" but also "of an age." The
English language was establishing itself as the dominant political
and cultural language of the island in Chaucer's time (in the last
major political event of Chaucer's life, the usurping Henry IV
claimed the throne with a speech in English). But he became a
poet in a world which was not only bilingual but trilingual, as
Gower acknowledged by writing his three major works in

French, Latin, and English, respectively. When Chaucer chose to write only in English although his early models were French, he made a major stylistic decision, and when he chose to execute ambitious and sophisticated structures in a language to which they were new, he was establishing a function for poetry in relation to the language of daily consciousness which is central to his distinctive achievement as a poet. The less successful the poetry of his contemporaries, the more light it sheds directly on this process; whereas the better it is and the less the apparent resemblance, the more it tells us about the factors he tried to bring to bear on each other and, indirectly, about the functions served by the structures he evolved or borrowed from non-English traditions.[1]

CONFESSIO AMANTIS

Chaucer dedicated *Troilus and Criseyde* to his friends "moral" Gower and "philosophical" Strode, but when Chaucer and Gower were linked by their contemporaries and successors as the "source and foundation" of poetry in English,[2] it was not for the scope of their thought. Rather, they were praised for rescuing English from the marketplace and transforming this limited, practical medium of daily life and popular entertainment into an instrument of expression capable of the heights to which great poets had raised other languages. In fact, Chaucer reserved the term "poet" for the continental tradition from Homer to Dante and called himself and his English contemporaries "makers." Chaucer and Gower are indeed close linguistically, in their models and sources, and in their verse form, at least until Chaucer abandoned the French-derived octosyllabic couplet for the pentameter line. The *Confessio Amantis* was written concurrently with Chaucer's *Legend of Good Women* and the beginning of the *Canterbury Tales,* and revised as Chaucer did his last work on them. Consequently it is entirely valid to compare Gower's work with Chaucer's and to let Gower's simplicity of style and decorative intricacy of structure throw into relief the range of Chaucer's style, the complexity of his narrative voice and poetic

[1]So short and general an essay cannot attempt the survey of information a literary history provides, nor adequately acknowledge the extent of its debt to other critics. The bibliography at the end of this volume tries to supply the lack.

[2]Caroline F. E. Spurgeon, *Five Hundred Years of Chaucer Criticism and Allusion* (Cambridge: at the University Press, 1925), I, 49.

structure, the scope of his mind, and the probing quality of his approach to the themes they have in common.

It is still for his creation of an urbane, clear, and flexible narrative manner that Gower is most often praised. He is preeminently the poet of the "plain style" which C. S. Lewis describes so engagingly. Lewis notes the near impossibility of appreciating what an achievement its sheer evenness represents or of doing justice to narrative "so spare, so direct, so concentrated on the event," adding rather less engagingly that Gower "stands almost alone in the centuries before our Augustans in being a poet perfectly well bred."[3] It is precisely because this style is so limpid that Gower's tales suffer even more than Chaucer's from being read, as they usually are, out of context.

Like Chaucer, Gower frames his tales in an elaborately presented dramatization of their telling which is as much a part of their point as the tales themselves, so that there are always two interacting levels of discourse. Gower's framework begins with a survey of contemporary England, lamenting the degeneration of individual, state, and church, which have fallen away from cosmic harmony into lesser, destructive modes of love. (This prologue may be seen as an abstract and much weaker analogue to the portrait series in Chaucer's *General Prologue*.) A dream vision then begins, in which a Dreamer clearly identified with the poet meets Venus and her priest Genius, as Chaucer's dreamer once met Alceste and the God of Love. The Dreamer is an aging lover courting a young girl, and Venus hands him over to Genius for cross-examination and advice. This "Lover's Confession," which gives the poem its name, proceeds according to the seven deadly sins as they apply to love, and Genius illustrates each point elaborately with stories. But by the end, the process has not turned the Dreamer into a successfully trained lover and courtier; rather, it has brought him to the recognition that he is too old to be a lover at all or to find in allegiance to a finite good his school of harmony and truth. Harmony with the larger order, the cosmic love whose violation was lamented in the prologue, must take the place of erotic passion however crafted and civilized. The poem, most of which celebrates so charmingly and with such businesslike optimism an "honeste love" that integrates the values of courtly passion with those of nature and ethics, ends, as it began, in a lament for time and change and for the incompatibility

[3] *The Allegory of Love*, (New York: Oxford University Press, 1936; reprinted New York: Galaxy Books, 1958), pp. 209, 202.

of good with good. Thus the overall structure is anything but simpleminded, and the individual stories take on more complex qualities in this larger plot with which they are in counterpoint if not in tension.

Both the *Confessio* and the *Canterbury Tales* are built concentrically, embedding simpler units in larger, formal ones, a kind of structure Burrow calls "encapsulation" and considers as characteristic of English art of this period as the interlacing of separate plots is of the continent.[4] Both use as their basic units stories—even some of the same stories—of the interaction between men and women in society, especially in different kinds of love stories. These, because of their parallelism, provide a sort of laboratory of the ways in which life may be exploited, or understood, or crafted, or enobled. Further, their subject matter links each concrete instance to the long-established and increasingly complex medieval tradition of analyzing the meanings of love. Each instance finds itself implicitly placed on a spectrum that ranges from the Venus who symbolizes the coherence and harmony of the universe, or the unpossessive love that resembles God's; through the Venus who exemplifies the fertility, variety, and cyclic renewal of the natural world, including humanity; to the Venus who embodies the psychological forces, sometimes ennobling and sometimes destructive, of human erotic experience, with all its social complications.

To analyze these interrelationships, the French tradition had turned to the personification allegory. But Chaucer and Gower, like Dante, looked for a kind of narrative in which individual people and situations could be presented directly and their implications brought out and correlated not in direct statement within the dramatization but through an analytical framework. Gower keeps a foot in both camps by retaining personification in the frame, and reduces instead of exploiting the potential complexity of his material both in the stories and in the overt explanations of the frame. He keeps to explicit, practical, and universally applicable meaning that is the intellectual equivalent of his smooth and unassuming style, never risking chaos or ambiguity, nor rising to tragedy or wisdom. Lucid narrative in the stories meets lucid formula in the frame, and whatever awareness the frame would be unable to accommodate is eliminated before it can arise in the stories by the style. In Chaucer, on the other hand, both levels

[4]J. A. Burrow, *Ricardian Poetry* (New Haven: Yale University Press, 1971), p. 68.

are equally fully dramatized and both equally devoid of formulated meaning at all adequate to exhaust the implications of the stories and their tellers or to make the process of relating experience to familiar intellectual and artistic patterns easy or clear. When Chaucer and Gower have used the same story, the difference between them is the clearest, especially in the case of the *Wife of Bath's Tale* and the *Tale of Florent* since here we also have two popular romance treatments of the story for comparison.[5] The "encapsulated" structure permits Chaucer to communicate more by juxtaposition than could be formulated directly; in Gower's hands it becomes a delightful puzzle, a masterpiece of the fluid Gothic tracery of fourteenth-century English windows, which makes the epithet which their contemporary, the French poet Deschamps, attached to Chaucer more applicable to Gower "grand translateur."

PIERS PLOWMAN

Piers Plowman is the polar opposite of the *Confessio*. Wherever experience and meaning fail to overlap tidily, Gower mutes experience and diffuses it into a formal pattern of order; whereas *Piers Plowman* takes the tension between them as its subject, and jettisons lucidity of style or argument with the greatest gusto wherever it would prevent the poem's action from plunging the reader headlong into the problems of relating them. As no other poem has ever done, it actualizes in profoundly moving if not always clear dramatic terms the process of trying to be an individual, a citizen, and a Christian without jettisoning the essence of any of these.

Piers Plowman, or, more properly, "Will's Vision of Piers the Plowman, with the Life of DoWell, DoBetter and DoBest," is the name given to one of the great riddles of literary history. Three strikingly different versions of this poem exist, whose composition covers roughly the same period as Chaucer's work (1362, 1377, and the early 1390s are characteristic guesses about the dates of the versions). The "B" and "C" versions are three times as long as "A" and attempt, by revision and by adding new action and discussion, to work out the implications of the A-text's powerful and often enigmatic story. Argument about whether

---

[5]These are all printed (but without the Gower frame) in W. F. Bryan and Germaine Dempster, eds., *Sources and Analogues of Chaucer's* Canterbury Tales (London, 1941; reprinted New York: the Humanities Press, 1958).

they were written by the same man dominated criticism of the poem from the turn of the century until quite recently, but by now the great majority of scholars feel that assuming several poets does not explain the poems' pecularities any better and makes their existence and their distinctive way of approaching experience even harder to account for. Nothing that is both certain and useful is known, however, about the "William Langland" to whom the poems are attributed except, for what it may be worth, what they say about the Dreamer, "Will."[6]

Piers Plowman is a dream vision and a personification allegory, written in alliterative verse, though not with the aristocratic complexity nor the special diction used by the *Pearl*-poet. A series of connected visions by a Dreamer explicitly said to be writing the poem combine brilliant satire on contemporary society with an analysis of the process by which the individual soul and the society in history may perfect themselves in the light of the eternal values which underlie and explain the world as we know it. Consequently the poem is not only a ruthlessly prophetic denunciation of present evils but a reenactment and rediscovery of the meaning of Christian teaching. It becomes as troubling an encounter with religious experience as any we find in a post-Christian society, but totally different in character because it is predicated on an acceptance of the very medieval Christian ideas which it is putting to the test (not, however, of the condition of the medieval church whose corruption and incompetence the poet, like so many others in his time, attacked with all the virulence we associate with the Reformation). The poem reflects a consciousness able to face from within the medieval world view precisely the problems others did not face until it had broken down. Furthermore, the poet is as aware of political, economic, and social dimensions of the problem as he is of psychological and religious ones, which gives his analysis sophistication to the same degree that it increases its complexity.

That the poem exists in three puzzlingly different versions is no coincidence but a reflection of its essential character. Its daunting complexity, frequent clumsiness, and apparently contradictory changes result from the poet's attempt to use an essentially conservative literary form and the intellectual and religious idiom of his day to confront human experience at a level to which they can be adapted only at the price of constant tension. Thus

[6]See George Kane, Piers Plowman: *The Evidence for Authorship* (London; the Athlone Press, 1965).

the poem involves the reader in an encounter that seems at times as demanding and painful for him, though also as illuminating and moving, as the poet himself seems to have found the writing of the poem. In fact, in complete contrast to any explicit medieval discussion of art known to us, *Piers Plowman* seems to reflect a mind driven almost against its will to use the creation of poetry as part of a process of discovery; indeed the Dreamer even goes so far, finally, as to defend the writing of the poem on precisely these grounds (B-text, XII, 1–29).

It would seem impossible for a work of art to have less in common with Chaucer. (Perhaps if Chaucer is the definition of poetry, we will have to call *Piers Plowman* something else.) More specifically, Chaucer, for all his acuteness in observing guildsmen's silver-mounted knives or corrupt pardoners' effect on the Church, leaves the relation between his work and the events of his age almost entirely implicit. How could an administrator and public servant, near whose very home over Aldgate the Essex peasants massed before the mobbing of London in the Peasants' Revolt, refer to this crucial event only once, and that comically? Chaucer is so reticent and embodies his themes in such natural-looking portrayals of individuals, however typical, that we find little guidance as to how we may legitimately use our knowledge of contemporary developments as a context for his poems. Hindsight shows us the staggering implications of the changes taking place in fourteenth-century England and the tragic conflict and loss, as well as danger and suffering, they entailed. But what kind of awareness can we say was possible from within the situation, and what factors in it could a medieval observer identify and appreciate? *Piers Plowman* is unquestionably atypical in the lengths to which the poet was prepared to go to do justice to the dislocations of the age and to recover a basis for belief and for social order. His peculiar brand of radical conservatism may be idiosyncratic. But the poem is invaluable in showing us what a sufficiently keen mind, grounded in theological, political and artistic tradition, could grasp and understand; what tragic pressure was exerted on contemporary consciousness; and how far an original intellect could carry its concern for the relationship between knowledge, experience, and poetry. Nothing could be more illuminating as a background for Chaucer's troubled analysis of art, illusion, and language and the complexities of his attitude toward Christian dogma and traditional ethics.

Likewise, Langland's attempts to find more satisfactory

combinations between social realism and allegorical analysis shed a great deal of light on Chaucer's deceptively "natural" narrative methods. Langland offers a wide range of combinations between direct imitation of social behavior and consciously analytical, intellectual perspective on that behavior. These range from discursive commentary on an issue uttered by speakers within a scene, through scenes that mix personifications with "real" people, to diagrammatic or emblematic scenes that symbolize the relationships between factors which the poem has presented more realistically or commented on more explicitly elsewhere. Again and again scenes in *Piers Plowman* parallel more realistic scenes in Chaucer—the contrast between the prologues of *Piers Plowman* and of the *Canterbury Tales* is only the most obvious example. At first sight, the comparison merely underlines the absence of overt allegory in Chaucer, as if Langland has two levels of action and Chaucer only one. But, in fact, closer comparison reveals the presence of formal elements in Chaucer as well, which deflect us from participation to analysis and direct that analysis. The difference is (as we noted in connection with Gower) that the analytical level presents us with nothing definitive either, and in its turn, deflects the mind back to the concrete. What resolution is offered must be picked up by the reader from the interaction of the two kinds of awareness, both incomplete.

THE PEARL-*POET*

No Middle English poems besides Chaucer's have been as admired and appreciated, since their rediscovery in the nineteenth century, as the four poems, *Pearl, Patience, Cleanness* (also called *Purity*), and *Sir Gawain and the Green Knight,* which occur in a single manuscript of about 1400 and are thought to be the work of one man, a contemporary of Chaucer who probably wrote for an aristocratic court in the northwest Midlands.[7] Generically, they are highly diverse—two biblical paraphrases involving totally different kinds of structure, one superb Arthurian romance, and one dream vision—but all are written in

[7]They surfaced when *Gawain* was published in 1839 and the whole group in 1864. A fifth poem, *St. Erkenwald,* in another manuscript, may be his; in any case, the five poems offer the best context for the study of each.

the most elaborate, subtle, and sophisticated form of alliterative poetry, often with rhyming elements as well.[8] Dates can only be deduced from the poems themselves, except to place the group in the later fourteenth century; the biblical poems, *Cleanness* and *Patience,* surely precede the far richer and longer *Gawain* and *Pearl,* and the thematic kinship of *Patience* with them, as well as the fact its structure is more complex than that of *Cleanness* even though it is shorter, probably makes *Cleanness* the earliest.

The alliterative tradition involves both a verse form and a style. Both the meter itself (of the four main stressed words in a line, the first three alliterate and the last should not) and a special vocabulary of poetic diction and of traditional alliterating phrases for all kinds of recurrent things and situations go back to Old English and beyond, and originally made possible the oral composition of poetry. The style did not die out with the Norman Conquest, but we have little record of the stages it went through before emerging, having adapted itself to the changes in the language, in the so-called Alliterative Revival of the later fourteenth century. Alliterative poetry demands an audience familiar with the tradition if it is to be understood at all. More important, the listener must be able to appreciate how a particular poet is using and diverging from past craftsmanship, just as a trained ear follows the patterns of Bach or Mozart, or the eye sees the difference between a great dancer or diver and a mediocre one in the performance of a recognizable unit of motion. Marie Borroff points out, for example, that in *Gawain,* "poetic" and "nonpoetic" language are played against each other within the individual line, since the poet uses the traditional alliterative vocabulary for the alliterating words but turns to emphatically nontraditional vocabulary for the fourth, nonalliterating stress. Such effects do not require a literate audience, nor a one-class audience like some elite poetry of the Renaissance, but they do demand a community of initiates and connoisseurs. We notice at once that they make the *Pearl*-poet much harder going for us, at least at first, than Chaucer or Langland; we do not always realize that he was just as difficult for any contemporary who was not a member of that community, which had once been coextensive with the whole

---

[8]*Gawain* separates long verse "paragraphs" with a rhyming "bob and wheel," and *Pearl's* stanzas are rhymed and linked in what may be the most constricting verse form ever used for narrative.

society but was now shrunk to a self-conscious culture within it, a "fit audience though few" to which Chaucer almost certainly did not belong.

The *Pearl*-poet is difficult for other reasons as well. His basic dialect is far removed from Chaucer's (and from ours) in grammar, syntax, and vocabulary (the strange words which are high poetic diction and the strange words that are local colloquial low style look alike strange to us). He seems to have consciously enriched this regional language with borrowings from courtly French and from Old Norse. Above all, he is the poet who pushed the possibilities of the alliterative style to their utmost limits, demanding but also rewarding the most intense and concentrated perception of which his audience is capable. He may well be the only Middle English poet whose language, especially in *Pearl,* has the density of texture, the complex suggestiveness within lyric intensity, the multileveled, structurally essential image patterns to which we must respond both associatively and intellectually, which Eliot and Yeats have taught us to look for as "the" language of poetry. Ordinarily, trying to read medieval poems this way is self-defeating: it merely focuses our attention on elements which are comparatively sparsely distributed and secondary in function, so that we miss the primary relationships between parts and the suggestiveness that are really there but attained by very different means. Chaucer's complexities are carried in solution, as it were, in a style whose overtly straightforward statement (plain or decorated) is the focus for the implications of its successively larger narrative contexts which the reader must bring to bear on it. Hence the possibility of disagreement among readers as to what, if any, meanings besides the obvious are "really there" and the unlikelihood that they will all merely reinforce each other and add up to sheer epic grandeur (hence also the persistency with which Matthew Arnold's criticism that Chaucer "lacks high seriousness" keeps being resurrected).

As long as our insufficient experience of Middle English makes it all sound a little odd and naive, we will be unable to trust our eye for this sort of effect. In some ways, the best corrective is to experience the *Pearl*-poet's opposite kind of suggestiveness. Whether at his most comic or his most tragic, he always writes like the jeweller whose image he uses for the narrator of *Pearl*. The civilized and splendid artifice he embodies and celebrates, in which he seeks a resolution for all the conflicting truths he brings to bear on the human condition, is always the poem's overt means as well as a part of its subject. His concern for perfection of form might seem an escape from the problems of his time; Charles Muscatine has called him "a man for whom the perfection of his art has become a kind of defense against crisis."[9] But if we consider the poems in order of increasing complexity, we see that sophistication and elaboration of form develop in parallel with more and more profound ethical and psychological concern, style reflecting more and more sharply the thematic concern for the gap between the ideal, summed up in God, and the finite reflected in human history. Perfection of form is his laboratory, the necessary condition of his greatest insight. It is as if he could move freely only in a straitjacket. It cannot be coincidence that *Pearl*, the one of his poems whose language reaches the highest degree of density and suggestiveness, is also the poem whose form is so demanding that one wonders he was able to use it for narrative at all.

Indeed, the conflicting meanings of art and artifice connect the poems thematically as well as in their imagery. In *Cleanness*, the splendid artifice of an aristocratic household, in which every aspect of life is brought together into a living work of art, is used as a way of defining that other perfection we call moral, which he pictures as not only the necessary human correlative of God's perfection but as self-evidently the only desirable life, obviously attainable by anyone who will bring to the process of living the same deliberate choices and developed skill that a craftsmen brings to his or her work. As Elizabeth Keiser shows, in this image every kind of good is fully congruous with every other, as well as with human beings' truest perception of their real nature, and of the nature of things in general. Here grace is just like everything people of true intelligence and cultivated sensibility like best.[10]

The other poems, however, reflect an increasingly tragic sense of the gap between divine perfection and the human order, between the splendor of absolute good and the finitude and fallibility of even the best knights or artists during their sojourn in history. The aristocratic image comes to seem as ironically diver-

[9] *Poetry and Crisis in the Age of Chaucer* (Notre Dame and London: Notre Dame University Press, 1972), p. 69.

[10] Elizabeth B. Keiser, "Perfection and Experience: The Celebration of Divine Order and Human Sensibility in *Cleanness* and *Patience*," unpublished dissertation, Yale University, New Haven, 1972.

gent from what humanity actually experiences of chivalry or kingship as the purchasable fourteenth-century pardon is from God's. Increasingly, the poet creates contexts in which this awareness is brought home to us by being demonstrated through a consciousness within the poem, who journeys away from, then home to a situation in the finite world. There alone, if anywhere, the unfinished character of the human search for perfection can find completion in God's response, whether He spares Nineveh, creates a household of "homly hyne" through bread and wine, or, crowned with thorns, reveals His lordship of history through "courteisie," not conquest. The *Pearl*-poet was somehow able to accommodate his consciousness to the vast universe revealed when he, like so many nominalist philosophers of the period, saw the gulf between the world of the human sojourn and the absoluteness of God's being. Human fallibility and limited perspective fall into place in a larger order where sufficiency and total splendor are God's alone. Thus perceived, humanity's tragic fallibility can be, like the Fall itself, a *felix culpa,* a "happy fault," and tragedy is subsumed into a glorious comedy. Here human beings can be, as A. C. Spearing describes so well, undignified, vulnerable, incomplete, and funny, because it is not they that sustain the world;[11] and the world can become, as it does most of all in *Gawain,* a glorious festival, a great game or dance in which the divine perfection, without losing any of its absolute exigency, reconciles the finite with itself in a loving reciprocity for which the courtly household of *Cleanness,* in spite of the poem's sociological and religious naïveté, was an almost perfect image. The poet's *oeuvre,* like each poem but one, returns enriched to its starting point.

To resolve tragedy without denying it, by setting conflicting elements into largely implicit relation with each other within an overall comedy, seems to have been Chaucer's intention too, especially in the *Canterbury Tales*. It is much harder, though, to be sure of the direction he was moving in, since many of the later tales show an increasingly frightening sense of humanity's demonic potential and present damage, since his pattern is far more diverse as well as unfinished, and since the *Retractions* scarcely suggest that he was of one mind about the project. Both men understood the perspective in which a thing can be all the more serious for being comic as well. Though they seem the farthest

[11]A. C. Spearing, *The Gawain Poet: A Critical Study* (Cambridge: at the University Press, 1970).

apart in almost every specific way, they are profoundly akin in being the poets who wrote the comedy of our tragedy, not by achieving Dante's intellectual lucidity and rigor but by rendering immanent in humanity's perception of all the varieties of its experience a larger perspective communicating more than can be said directly.

CHAUCER AND "ORDINARY LANGUAGE": NARRATIVE, LYRIC, AND DIDACTIC FORMS

We are left with the problems raised by Chaucer's use of the bad English poetry of his day. It is here that several recent studies of Chaucer have markedly affected our approach to his narrative method. Chaucer chose to write in English at a time when popular art forms were proliferating as a larger and larger middle-class audience became patrons of vernacular entertainment and edification. Some of this literature developed from native traditions, some involved the adaptation (or the butchering) of continental models. But all reflect a transition from the aristocratic, or at least manorial, household, which had been the original fostering ground of vernacular literature, to more diverse and often less sophisticated consumers of "sentence" and "solas," preferably in combination. That Chaucer used the romance, the lyric, the sermon, and the proverb has always been obvious because his parody of them is overt. But critics used to resurrect the worst romances merely to make the point that Chaucer laughed at them. Only recently have we been asking ourselves why Chaucer, who never minded leaving continental influences, from good and bad poetry alike, perfectly identifiable, was so selective about his English contemporaries. He allows the bad and the slight to leave unmistakable marks on his poems while apparently maintaining as total a detachment from the best minor works like *Sir Orfeo* as from the major poems or from the specific events of fourteenth-century history. As Burrow observes of the most obvious parody, *Sir Thopas,* "the relationship between *Thopas* and the rest of Chaucer's work is more equivocal, and much more interesting, than it appears at first sight."[12]

Several critics have pointed out how many of the basic features of the seldom admired Middle English romance are to be found in Chaucer's most distinctive work, quite apart from the

[12]*Ricardian Poetry,* p. 15.

mindless or clumsy aspects he parodies. D. S. Brewer argues that
what differentiates Chaucer from his continental models is, above
all, a narrative strategy and style which "resides in the language
as it had been spoken and evolved for nearly a thousand years,
and in that artistic formulation of the language which is found
in . . . the Middle English rhyming romances."[13] These elements, which we tend to overlook amid the sheer bulk of incident,
include brisk handling of action, exchanges in short dialogue,
telling and selective concrete detail (but not in catalogs and formal description), and a tone of humane realism interspersed
through a plot and an imaginary world unrealistic enough to be
completely flexible and, in the best romances, richly symbolic.
These stories also reflect an accommodation between "courtly
love" and the ideas of marriage and family.[14] Most important of
all, their language and conventions express the poet's relation to
his audience in terms of teller and listener, a narrative mode
which, in Chaucer as in the other major Middle English poets,
became fictionalized and provided the central structuring device
of long and complex narratives. These important contributions do
little to enliven modern reading of most of these romances, but an
excellent example of the popular romance that remains anything
but boring is *Ywain and Gawain*. A "translation" of Chrétien de
Troyes's *Yvain,* it finds little favor with Francophiles since it
sacrifices all the characteristic excellences of its source except
the intricate plot. But, in so doing, it achieves an unassumingly
admirable narrative mode, epitomizing what Burrow calls "the
vigorous wild stock upon which were grafted Chaucer's other,
more literary and sophisticated styles."[15]

Is it simply that later tradition has made us so used to this
sort of thing when it is done well that we only stop to identify the
source when the bad rather than the good is being imitated? We
must note that the same problem is presented by Chaucer's use of
the other popular forms. The fourteenth-century lyric was not
characteristically the elaborately crafted structure we find in the
earlier Harley lyrics. Long didactic, religious pieces abound,
along with the songs, especially love songs, to which Chaucer
makes reference and whose shopworn vocabulary he demoted

[13]"The Relationship of Chaucer to the English and European Traditions,"
Chaucer and Chaucerians, D. S. Brewer, ed. (University, Ala.: University of
Alabama Press, 1966), pp. 3–4, 10.

[14]Gervase Mathew, *The Court of Richard II* (London: Murray, 1968), pp.
129–37.

[15]*Ricardian Poetry,* p. 21.

from serious narrative to ironic use.[16] Chaucer is usually described as comparatively poor at lyric. But this criticism refers to his separate short pieces. If we consider instead the lyrics written for his characters to say in dramatized situations, which, in the *Canterbury Tales,* usually follow more familiar native and biblical traditions rather than French and Italian models, we find none of that Augustan reserve which makes his ballades best where they are least lyric and most humorous or didactic. The same principle applies to the sermon. The fourteenth-century sermon—we recall that sermons were among the Wife of Bath's favorite forms of entertainment—is more than a source for the background ideas of the age. It was a hatching ground for important styles of short narrative, especially for social observation and satire, a feature whose influence on Langland has attracted more attention than on Chaucer. The sermon was the most generally accessible model for ordered discourse and purposive argument. Its *exempla* provided a tradition of narratives whose *"sententia,"* or further meaning, was not allegorical but rather a natural extension of its overt meaning. But ordinarily it is only when the fact that a character is preaching a sermon or using distinctively clerical arguments in the point of a tale that we consciously note the influence of preaching.

Chaucer's use of the proverb illustrates perhaps the most clearly how Chaucer used all familiar English styles. Proverbs and collections of proverbs flourished in England and had played a role in sophisticated verse at least since *The Owl and the Nightingale*. But no reader, however unfamiliar with them, can overlook a proverb because the point of a proverb is to sound different from the surrounding language—different stylistically because different psychologically and philosophically. It identifies itself as the kind of statement that relates the speaker to the common experience in a specific kind of way. The proverb user is consciously turning to language for a means of aligning himself with the community's pragmatic, cautionary, and conservative insight on controlling the chaos of life. (We note that proverbs apply anywhere, since they usually come in pairs that recommend opposite solutions.) "A stitch in time" is usually quoted after the stitch was not taken and the nine proved necessary. Our mistake about Chaucer's proverbs is not overlooking them but taking them for his considered wisdom rather than as part of the be-

[16]E. Talbot Donaldson, "The Idiom of Popular Poetry in the Miller's Tale" (1950); reprinted in *Speaking of Chaucer* (New York: Norton, 1970), pp. 13–29.

havior of a speaker who is using them in some decorative or useful counterpoint to a situation, often in a tacit admission of futility.

Unless we become familiar enough with what was ordinary language of one or another sort for Chaucer's audience if not for him (an awareness which comes from reading poems, not from parallel passages in the notes of a Chaucer text), we will miss one of the most important aspects of the *Canterbury Tales*. Chaucer has created a network of language, styles, and genres as familiar and definable as the sociological styles of the pilgrims and just as concrete, fascinating, and problematic. These styles are as integral to the functions the mind exercises to come to terms with its environment as the distinctive clothes, manners, and work in which Chaucer was so interested are to life in society and even more revealing of the central issues of human existence. Precisely because these styles are recognizable ones, Chaucer has created a world peopled with languages as surely as did J. R. R. Tolkien. (It cannot have been coincidence that *The Lord of the Rings* was written by a medievalist.)

We can see why it was of the very essence of Chaucer's poetic enterprise that his exploration of human consciousness within a world of other people should be written in English: English was the language of daily experience and awareness; of weak or dangerous ways of representing one's experience to one's self and others, as well as of vital and illuminating ones. Securely rooted in actuality, it was just in the process of defining itself as a medium for the high awareness of great art and sophisticated intellectual systems, philosophical and religious. The familiarity of English gives an underlying vigor and simplicity to the analytical concerns that came to Chaucer from earlier French poetry, especially *Le Roman de la Rose*. The familiarity of specific styles—hence his fondness for the most stereotypically recognizable ones—dramatizes the process by which the characters, and ultimately the poet himself, articulate their experience within an existing language and existing forms, to arrive at an accommodation between the experience and the patterns and truths which surround it.

The recognizability of styles is also the key to Chaucer's ability to confront complex meaning without being reduced to Langland's moving, but so often unilluminating, condition. Readers must become as much connoisseurs of styles, good and bad, as the *Pearl*-poet's audience was of its own tradition. Then they will be able to see, in the execution of the effect recognizably being attempted by the speaker in any given passage, limitations and variations which deflect their attention outward to the position of the passage in the narrative, to what (if anything) we know of the speaker, to the immediate and the larger narrative context, to the values associated with this particular style or with this intellectual position, to parallel but divergent situations within the work, to relevant literary models, and to the narrative voice behind all these. From some or all of these, depending on what proves appropriate to the passage, the reader will return with heightened awareness of it. The sum total of these distinct awarenesses—which are "in" the passage in the sense that it evokes them, but which are not included within its own language or content—when synthesized by the reader, is the impact of the passage. (If Burrow, when he calls this a "middle-aged" style, means that a considerable amount of living is required before we can fully appreciate it, he is quite right.) Even where Chaucer's satirization of familiar language is most obvious, it is ambivalent, part of an exploration of the function such styles, and better ones as well, serve. It is of the essence of his insistence on working with limited narrators. "Diverse folk diversely they seyde" is as much the subject of the *Canterbury Tales* as its means.

Stavros Deligiorgis

Poetics of Anagogy for Chaucer: the Canterbury Tales

> *The story told by Aristomenes was so delightful that I realized we reached our destination as much by my horse's back as by my ears.*—
> Apuleius, *Met., ad init.*

If "Chaucer" is a pilgrim in the *Canterbury Tales,* we must be too. We are educated into the ordinary, we listen to it, we take sides, we forget, while the troupe plods onwards to the shrine of the martyr saint. The *General Prologue* smoothly assumes the limits of its external audience. Readers and listeners are shown only intermittently concerned or prepared to like and understand all the performances; the rhetoric of the notorious "gallery," the expanded portraits, on the one hand, and the compressed, combined allusions, on the other, make of us one of them. The primary narrator keeps us classically unbored. Some names and qualities are spun out, but then there are names and professions that are barely hinted at, the latter seeming to vary the proverbial monotony of the former, but clearly ensuring our future confirmations that some of the pilgrims "spoke" exactly as introduced; guaranteeing our disappointment in the characters who promised but did not deliver; our surprises at the good performances from characters who were scarcely mentioned during the introductions. As consumers of literature we insist on and impose a world limited by ordinary awareness, inertia, and passivity. In our acceptance of the logic and the organization of the opening of the poem, we lead the unthinking lives of the fiction in human form we go to the poem for. We may be a bit less violent and vulgar, but we are as idle and as much the cause of our dullness as any of the storytellers. Taken severally, the speakers satisfy secondary realism. Stories, to the adaptive, popular explanation, make time pass. The work *plus* ourselves suggests that there is no Canterbury apart from the tales (the *canti* as well as the recanting) told in its anticipation. Living hydraulically, we find it rather hard to draw in and identify with the totality of the travelers in the *General Prologue*. But there is always Aristotle, unfortunately: the ranks, the professions, the sexes, the paths of life are there to justify literature in various styles and genres which, thanks to neoclassical rumor, we know how to receive. We are so eager to see the epic in the first tale of the collection and to match it really against the portrait of the Knight, we turn Aristotle so fast, we turn that first tale into the paradigm of the literature of conventions. We feel presented with a certain concept of entertainment!

The alternative is an active, willful career of our own as fictions with the *Tales* reading us. Of course we bore them; we have nowhere to go. We may have identified the classicizing epic hint in Latin prefacing the *Knight's Tale,* but we have forgotten or ignored Canterbury and the martyr's body (to be found over and over, in every fit, between the showers' piercing of the root of the drought to the Cook's drunken fit at the other end of the collection). Only the grammatological saves us in the eyes of our literary readers, and our awareness that they are made, unlike our discrete constitution, concurrently of spatial and temporal pulsants; of sounds in a half-known language that exists only to affect deeply and substantively what we may ever apprehend as theme; of logical, programmatic exposition that is not undercut by contradictory execution. We clothe the text with the matter of our reading, we flesh it with the morality of all human beauty, and we require the holy martyr's cardinal fix from then on continuously. When we realize that phonetic approximations also lead to flashy *gestalten,* we have begun planning, methodically, our own formation.

Before repressing the degree to which we edit a text as we experience it, we repress the fact and the extent of our subjection to it. Our relation to it is not that of the recognition of exhibits; it is the assumption of certain types of introspection, certain tasks of self-discipline and, even, the embracing of unpleasantness in our acceptance of the "given" values with no hope of justification or compensation. In simple terms, and to deal specifically with the *Canterbury Tales,* we need to swallow and accept very early those silent "e's" long before we have seen the reasons for them in the rhyming couplets, and the narrator's privileged timings and brands of lucidity, continuity, or pointed digression; we are governed by his equations of the long poem with human, pathic unimaginativeness (the *Knight's Tale*); his collocation of the amusing or farcical with the familial and the domestic (the *Miller's* and the *Reeve's Tales*); his unstated but indubitable linking of rational judgment to the topical (in the lambasting of institutional imperfection; or of the orders, for example); and in his "typically medieval" conflating of the artistic talent (alluded to, for example, in singing, chanting, etc.) with the ecclesiastical (the *Prioress's tale*). We can say, at last, that we are on our way:

> The first city on the way to the fatherland . . . is Grammar. Its gate is the voice . . . the triple road . . . leading to the residences of precepts. Syllables . . . offer access to them. The city is divided in eight parts . . . corresponding to the eight parts of speech and the eight beatitudes of the soul. . . . In this city Donatus and Priscian teach the travelers a new language . . . and give them the clear instructions which will see them to the fatherland. The settlements which are subject to the city are the books of the poets, themselves divided into four areas: tragedies, comedies, satire, and the lyric. Tragedies—take Lucan's—deal with wars; comedies—e.g. Terence's—with matters of marriage; satire—Persius', for example—is about the objectionable; the lyric consists of odes— like Horace's—resounding and lauding gods and kings in hymning voice.[1]

The "first city" we just heard about implicates Chaucer in a peculiar way. He provides a set of paradigms whose reach and range we must be prepared to realize, yet as "a writer," he too must be on his way towards the fatherland. Objective, definitive, "scientific" (in the European sense) philology, especially by assuming that didactic literature is literature, raises poets first to the status of the other greats-on-the-road, then drops them into a specialized slot, almost in spite of the protestations of secondary criticism advancing a different classification. This is only right.

---

[1]This and the subsequent quotations are from a brief work by Honorius of Autun, d. 1136, *On the Banishment and Fatherland of the Soul, or, On the Arts.* Honorius Augustodunensis, *De animae exsilio et patria, alias De artibus, Patrologia Latina,* 172, cols. 1242–46; translations by the author.

Good criticism is not literary or esthetic. It is, rather, like the art it countenances. It risks impressionism and both replaces and posits its occasion. Rhetoric, obviously, begins here as a condition. The epideictic, the hortatory, and the forensic are taken, persistently, to make words out of things for some reason or another. The jumble of forms in the *Canterbury Tales* frustrates the game of matching styles to plots (words to things?). Rhetoric, then, is language approximately as an encyclical is theology. One listens and attends to clerical exposition very much because one believes, not that one may believe. Chaucer's footing on our Parnassus is the same as Demosthenes' (in his *Philippics*). The works were "effective" because we read them now. The reverse of this proposition is responsible for our sense of poetry as eloquence. Chaucer ought to suffice against this, all treatises to the contrary. When we are told, item by item, what we will not be told—in the most serious of contexts—when the question of human autonomy, for instance, is passed on to "the divines" for an answer, we the audience are partners of the poet, we are shown the seams, and we are spared the impressive *demonstrationes;* since, already thinking beyond themes, we will not be reaching, in Keats's phrase, irritatingly, after the "facts" but reading to be read; not read to. For the *Canterbury Tales'* dumb audiences are not us, they are certain parts of us that need an enormous amount of help:

> The second city through which one must go on the way to the fatherland is Rhetoric. Public responsibility is the entrance [which then leads] . . . to the triple thoroughfare of the demonstrative, deliberative, and judicial functions. The leaders of the Church compose decrees in one part of the city, kings and judges propound edicts in another. . . . [Cicero] instructs the travelers to the city in ornate speech, he also helps them by means of the four moral virtues of prudence, fortitude, justice and temperance. The subjects of this city are histories, fabulous narratives, compositions on oratory and ethics, through which [souls] are led to the fatherland.

With the admission of an inferior part in our constitution, we return to logic. It is there not to judge, compare, refute, or propound. Perhaps awareness of this problem may have fixed, already since Zeno's time, the relationship between dialectics and an agonistic, or a sense of contesting; the two of them making for excellent drama. And while everybody watching could stay interested and analytic, the gain would be on the level of the unspoken desire for an image. The *Pardoner's Tale* is dialectical—however cynical—to the end; the Host's explosion is the desired image, in itself less of a punishment than the victory of dialectics suggesting the checking game between statement and life, between the tale and its channel. Is this biographical criticism? The hunt after genuineness? Or rather an objection to the divulgence of the highest experience in mysticism? "Those fake relics, they are as good as the real ones; better, being un-special. Come worship, and leave your money. You will feel great." The authentic may be too deep for words, but not for fiction. The Host momentarily moralizes but later is reconciled to the Pardoner, and that is because forgiveness is a dialectic. The Host in his impatience is an average logician (and average critic); but he is a dialectician, which admits no qualifier, in his reconciliation; and, of course, a good man. Had he stayed on his high *indignatio,* he would be the classic mouther, as Theodor Adorno would have said, of the "authentic." Relativity may be only the notorious long view of dialectics, which implies that Plato's evildoers—or the unorthodox in Christianity—are ignorant not of any particulars that might affect them, but of the ultimate conformations that could easily see them through despair as well as through dead certainty. The audiences of a work are not the axiomatic purveyors of the long view; not even the internal audiences. The Pardoner, by willfully embracing and acknowledging deceit, earns the not-so-eventual grace of the Host. The two are one theme; *the* theme, and what makes as much "literature" of readers or listeners as they, in their passivity, make of it.

> Dialectics is the third city through which one must go on the way to the fatherland, a city fortified by questions. It receives the travelers through the five entrances of genus, species, difference, the substantive, and the accidental. . . . Those whom Aristotle accepts into [his] *Topics*, he trains in argumentation, and through the *Peri hermeniis* [*On interpretation*], leads into the field of syllogisms. In this city the travelers learn to oppose heretics by the use of the arms of reasoning.

Heterogeneity shows its face before character or plot. Like it, shaggy dog stories, "unfair" stories, offend deontological criticism; they expose, it seems, only the most mechanical limitations of an audience. Perhaps there are no other limitations, since objections to heterogeneity grow on the ground of the most mechanical kinds of ignorance exposed. Nevertheless, we are astonished that we stay attracted to the diversity, the confusions, the fumblings in Chaucer. Stately pieces thoroughly belabored; fillers admitted as such; learned allusions truly leaving humanity out; tales armored between Introductions, Prologues, and Epilogues; shards of French; prose tales; tales in couplets and in stanzas of every reputation; references to Old English, Breton originals, and the worlds of the Round Table; pun floats; mistaken cues; neat sequences, every transition thread in place; convulsive interceptions; inarticulateness and facility, all forming a gathering that is conscious and unconscious, visual and linguistic at the same time; logistical and grandly statistical; matter reminded of space. Not the crowding schoolmasters' fear. The opposite, rather. Depletion; the antinomies; or an older author's *rhythmimachia,* the clash or battle of rhythms:

> The road to the fatherland goes through the fourth city of Arithmetic. In it, with Boethius as an instructor, odd and even join one another. . . . By the use of the fingers . . . the abacus multiplies . . . divides . . . and reduces a unit . . . to thousandths. The contest of rhythms calls forth odd and even numbers to battle . . . ; it governs by numerical determination the competing sides of the game of chess. . . . In this city as a school the traveler learns that God disposes of everything in the form of measure, number and weight.

World order mesmerizes. We observe that we may cease observing. Mediation is still possible but only through the awesome changes of reprojection, the technique by which devout people entirely avoid fatalism. Fate "writes" or "paints" ahead of time (e.g., the death of Julius Caesar even before he is born, in the *Knight's Tale*); angels sing or blow trumpets; God walks the earth in disguise (as in the legend of Saint Julian, who is mentioned in the Franklin's portrait in the *General Prologue*), inspects and tests to his satisfaction. The macrocosm is only a microcosm, but this too is reversed. Dame Custance (in the *Man of Law's Tale*) at one point slowly begins to surface. But when precisely? With Dame Custance we allow forces and laws (constants?) much larger than us to work on us. We first had to submit to the tale; suffer willingly with Dame Custance as we suffered the rules of the narrative, before seeing the point of it all, before saving the work from its own inertia. And if Custance's reemergence takes time, if there are relapses, they may be but the drama of the audience's moments of wavering and doubt whether any pains ever got anybody anywhere. Aristotle in the *Poetics,* in the general discussion of tragedy as the imitation of an action, submits that music too is an imitation, but of the emotions of the audience! Brilliant and ingratiating, especially to the millions of the insecure intelligences of the West since the late Neolithic. Audiences, however, do become conscious of their contributions to the sources of their experiences:

> Music is the fifth city through which we must pass on our way to the fatherland. According to the teachings of Boethius, there is a choir of deep, male voices and . . . one of high pitched children's voices praising God. . . . In that city the travelers are taught by the modulation of their mores to reach and join the harmony of the heavens.

We have been reminded already of the calculating hand on the abacus, of the deep voices of men in song, and of syllogisms as armaments. Labels are listening. A merchant's wife and a hypocritical monk exchange francs for flanks while the merchant is away in Flanders! When the transaction is criticized, the wife asks for future scorings (!) on her "taille" (tail? tally?) which is echoed by the Shipman's own "taillyng ynough" from God to the end of our days. Accounts keep us safely within the worlds we must explore. The merchant of the *Shipman's Tale* exists between Saint Denis, Bruges, and Paris. Yet he is divided between his "sommes, bokes, and . . . rekenynges" his wife despises, and the real possibility of failing (or going on a pilgrimage!) which alone would show one the true face of the world (lines 216–36). The world of campaigns mentioned in the Knight's portrait in the *General Prologue,* however missionary, crusader, and Christian, spans all (the) three continents of the known world, yet scarcely satisfies the Knight, who joins a pilgrimage on the soil of England. In the case of the Knight we realize a notion lost to us now: geometry as geography. As for Aratus, the fact that modern readers find him "didactic," and the fact that Paul's one allusion (out of two others) to pagan writing is to him, make him only more valuable to the maturing of any cosmology.

> Our homeland is to be reached through the sixth city of Geometry. Aratus in it unfolds a map of the world and points to Asia, Africa, and Europe; he gives an account of the mountains, cities, and rivers . . . through which the travelers must pass.

The opening of *The Parson's Prologue* returns us to our original narrator who gives us the familiar time setting between the last words of the Manciple and the Host's exchanges with the Parson. We are reminded of sidereal fixes in other tales (e.g., the Franklin's, immediately preceding the moment when the lover, the brother, and the magician from Orleans literally descend on Dorigen's world), but we may begin to doubt whether they are all decor, or all astronomical/astrological lore Chaucer was showing off. During those moments in the narrative, we are directed to the various actions or patterns of action that the characters or the readers would not pay any attention to: the tones of the light, the shadows, the seasons, the state of the "green in every yard" (*FranklT,* 1251), the approaches to a village. Rather selfishly, we will feel in good hands, but the zodiacal, celestial, or terrestrial clues are followed up by the Parson's (Persoun's, in the conventions of Middle English) claims of provenance and the reasons for the kinds of literature not to be expected from him. The perspective is getting wider. Geography and poetry are closely related. And beyond them there is the very complex idea of what has already been fabulated on the way to the shrine at Canterbury. The Parson resembles the narrator in the relationships he sees between astronomy and history (the former carrying the latter); but he resembles the Host in his indifference to the known categories of literary analysis (he will tell no fable; he "says," in rhyme, that he can barely rhyme; promises, finally, a merry tale, which turns out neither merry nor talelike. He then announces a meditation, which the Host accepts and echoes). From the Old Testament quotation in Latin with which the Parson begins his performance, to the explication he supplies of the word *via* ("way" or "path") as "sentence" or precept, and the movement of the paths through penitence to Christ, he only expands the image of the pilgrimage towards the Heavenly Jerusalem which he evoked in his Prologue. There are two matters that should not slip by: the first is the Parson's wish that he be granted wit to show ". . . the wey, in this viage/ Of thilke parfit glorious pilgrymage/ That highte Jerusalem celestial" (lines 49–51); the wit is there already in the fulgurant joining of the way and its goal. The second is related: Hyginus, writing in the times of Augustus, arranged a book of countless compressed narratives, tragedies, myths, as well as whole romances of separation and reunion. The sky, directly or indirectly, was the limit. Title: *Poeticon astronomicon libri IV*.

> Astronomy is the seventh city on the way leading to the mansions of the fatherland. Hyginus in it demonstrates, using an astrolabe, the increments and decrements of the moon . . . the recurrent paths of the sun . . . he rolls a sphere showing the marvels of the zodiac. . . . Julius explains the computation by which years and realms are numbered. The heavenly bodies . . . incite the traveler to the praise of the Creator.

The short-lived mime of the Canon's Yeoman's haste to tell all does not explain the repetitive and cataloging vocabulary of the first section (e.g., poudres; armonyak; orpyment) and the dwelling on repeated actions in the latter one. Are we experiencing too the exuberance and release from the Canon's obsessive fraud? The Canon approaches, overhears, mumbles a threat, and then withdraws out of the hearing of his own well-known deeds, as we withdraw, unconsciously of course, with the help of the garrulous but righteous narrator, into positivism. The earliest comment concerning the Canon is that he is very wise and capable of paving the rest of the road to Canterbury with gold and silver. When the Canon's apparent poverty is mentioned, the aide shifts to paradox: he is *too* wise, therefore, he is an ignoramus. Two movements follow: the confession that the Canon and his assistant are swindlers and the story of *a* canon, not the pilgrim, who once deceived a priest. The doubly compounded fiction of the recessed Canon is criticized as much for deluding and exploiting an innocent, as for the ''Canon's'' interest in gold—however unsynthesizable—the root of human evil. This too we can follow. Through the ranting we cannot hear the quiet fact that the two dissimilar partners have joined the pilgrimage to the saint of Canterbury. The Canon's mien, on the other hand, may be suggesting a few alternatives to the Yeoman's tale. For as long as we are amused by the storyteller's ingenuousness, accept his condemnations of deceit and hypocrisy, his story is our story. The questioning tone that looks forward to nineteenth-century science, the doubting of the supernatural, the wish for reason and honesty will be heard repeatedly in the *Canon's Yeoman's Tale*. But something else will be heard also, which does as much for the other tales surrounding it as for the history of ideas. The names alone could give us a hint: secONDE NONNE; chaNOUNS yeMAN; MAUNciple; persOUN. Or, following our conventions, secOND NUN; caNON's yeoMAN; MANciple; parsON. Saussure (and Starobinski) would have seen the important ''hypo-gram'' to place next to Dante's acrostic man (VOM). Chaucer's human-interest sequence is no pap. Saint Cecilia stays alive in the fire bath (a *balneum mariae?*); the Canon sweats like a still (a "stillatorie"); he is dressed for protection against heat, his horse barely moving, covered with perspiration and flecks of foam; the Cook is in a stupor, falls off his horse, is accused of infecting the other pilgrims with the stench of his breath (which is, in turn, compared to hell), pitied for his drunken pallor, called a ghost and a carcass, yet earning, to the Host's philosophical delight, a homeopathic dose of the same spirits that got him down earlier.

The human drama of the prologues to the end of the *Canterbury Tales* provokes a questioning of the narratives that follow. We too equate alchemy with the de- or concoction of gold. We do not have to play Jung to change our minds. The activities in the alchemical lab in the first half of the tale are genuine activities; they are desperate, even mistaken, but they are no rehearsals for future cheatings. We catch a glimmer of frantic fumblings after a form of the promised elixir (Arabic article + Greek "xeron"), the key to the "dry" principle (as opposed to the moist) in everything that can suffer or disintegrate. The Philosopher's Stone and the Alchemist's Gold appear as synonyms of the control over dissolution and death. Alchemy for gain shows only an impoverished, literally, and degraded humanity; it is a lamentable proposition in comparison with the concept of a universe made up of the four classical elements (air, fire, earth, and water), manipulation of which was thought to lead to balanced states of health and vigor. Near the end of the tale, Plato is said to have known the "water . . . maad . . . of elementes foure," the "roote" of which he would not divulge. We are not very far from the root of drought with which the *General Prologue* starts. We may remember also that Doctour of Physik who, according to the narrator, was "grounded in astronomye," which affects the elemental potencies of everything on earth, therefore affecting the human condition through the minerals, the vegetable, and animal ingredients of prescribed diets and medication. The presentation ends on a note of sarcasm as the narrator mentions gold as a medicinal "cordial," which explains why the doctor loved gold "in special," and why, by stopping with the physical ("his studie was but litel on the Bible"), he would make an excellent victim of the Canon's Yeoman's fiction, not *our* Canon's who knocks himself and his horse out to go to Canterbury, and is glad he is on time.

The eighth city by which one must go to reach the homeland is physic[al science]. Hippocrates instructs travelers here in the nature and efficacy of herbs, trees, stones, and animals; he leads from the treatment of the body to the treatment of the soul.

The miraculous child in the tale of the Prioress leaves everybody awed. We may speak even of a metrical aftereffect. The Host's jokes that change the mood, together with the description of the general atmosphere, are all in the rhyme royal that the Prioress employed in her *conte devot*. The "Childe" is there in the tale Chaucer himself offers the company of pilgrims. Clearly one fiction is used for the broaching of another, even in the case that the latter would be the negation of the preceding one, or its qualification (to the extent we recognize a child-pretext in the *Tale of Melibee* as well). It is conceivable that Chaucer, in this triple sequence, was not merely showing his wares, but almost a triple certainty that he will be misread. The problem of literary contexts is enormous. Orpheus' talking head, the pomegranate seeds in the mouth of Persephone (in Ovid and the Homeric Hymn)—are they in the tale of the Prioress? Its stereotyped intolerance and its sentimentality suggest a tradition that had not yet seen itself from the outside; the Christian myth it erects (as inclusive and as bloody as any Oedipus, Atreus, or Thyestes) is genuine to the very question of its uses. Didactic? In a society that knew it already? Magical? in an age of rituals? Literary? to complement the liturgical? We may have the answer here why in *Sir Thopas* the auctorial sensibilities presume to fade into insignificance as one tale is "interrupted" to make room for another. One thing is certain, the replacement cannot, by any definition, be mistaken for textbook literature.

The Host is busy too. He diminishes the distance between "Chaucer," who looks "elvyssh" and who keeps his eyes on the ground ("as [he would] fynde an hare"), and Sir Thopas' dogged search to find the elf queen he had dreamed would sleep with him. Chaucer tells the Host that the story he will tell is a "rym he lerned longe agoon." It is a stylized "rym," no doubt, a genre "rym" which leads to the stylized youth of the protagonist, his comical, but dead-earnest amours erupting in the first person confessional, the postponed confrontation with Sir Olifaunt (elephant, naturally, but also ol-i[n]fant), background-arts arming scene, everything known and heard before: Fairye, Termagant, the *ecphrasis* of the precious clothes, saddle, harness, weapons, crest and helmet, the flower of chivalry, and every other hyperbole. The dilution of language, however, the fact that "Chaucer" and Thopas talk so similarly, beside the progressive numbing to hyperbole, clearly affect the potency of the paragons who are part of the mechanism of praise in the tale. Progressively, the degrading of the greats in the automatic comparisons (Horn, Lybeaux, etc.) is the degrading of one art taking down, in its fall, all the other arts, sumptual or functional, in ideas or in things. Chaucer in *propria persona* botching "unconsciously" the only literature that could be placed next to the Christian one within which the Prioress worked. Both the surface and the deeper workings of the tale are becoming visible simultaneously. Medieval romances are not destroyed by the criticism of a fiction, they are anabolized to critical software. They help us ask why catalogs work in one tale and not in another; why exaggeration gels into literature in one instance but not in another; why minimalism satisfies and does not satisfy. No one knows that characters, the action, or the setting are *ever* what they seem. Audiences are instructed that if they perceive anything it is their making. The prototypes abound: hunters turn to planners, agents are acted upon, preservers become the source of fruitfulness. A device in the ancient world, a *mêchanê,* also meant "a way out," "a means of escape," or a solution, we might add, to problems of unknown scale.

> The ninth city by which we may reach our fatherland is Mechanics. There travelers learn every kind of work with metals, wood, and marble, but also painting, sculpture and every art proceeding from the hands of man. There Nimrod erected his tower; here Solomon constructed his temple; here Noah built the ark.

We leave the tale of *Sir Thopas* to the beat of couplets and to the opinion that its narrator was "lewed," "drasty" of speech and rhyme. The promise of a moral tale follows, itself followed by a discussion of the concept of the variant. We are taken immediately to the four Gospels telling the same and yet not the same story. The *Tale of Melibee* that "Chaucer" is about to deliver (in prose) is related, for those who have heard a different version, to the question of the four Gospels, but really introducing the critical notion of intertextual structures. No sooner have we heard of the murderous attack on Melibee's wife and daughter than we hear the precepts of Ovid on the timing of consolation.

Every moment in the story is similarly enveloped, counter-pointed, divided, and rejoined by entire clusters of quotes from countless *auctours* who seem to have known the tale and its problem all along. Paul, Petrus Alfonsus, Solomon, the Evangelists, Cicero, Seneca, Cassiodorus, Gregory the Great, even the pamphlet of Pamphilus, spell amongst them the eventual disappointment we will experience in Melibee's final speech to his enemies. That should serve as reminder that the work exists somewhere between the *sentences* of Prudence's exhortations and a pervasive resistance to change, Melibee's hesitations, mis-givings, and ruminations. The latter, certainly, is beyond mere subject matter, if we think of it as a dramatization of the process of its composition. Melibee's emotions almost make it a tale of war. Dame Prudence's oratory does not simply address those emotions, it prevents its turning into a tale of revenge. In sum-mary, we may speak of the tale as what it does not become. This is therefore what we are left with: a final, public gesture with Melibee acting more and more like a dignitary rising to the point of accepting the contrition of his enemies, and blessed with a shrewd counsellor; a defensive, or reactive pose (however eloquent and sincere) that would be embarrassed by the reminder that the attack upon his home happened while Melibee "for his desport [had gone] into the feeldes hym to pleye"; Prudence, the victim of a beating, soothing and comforting Melibee rather than the other way round.

The central impulse throughout is, precisely, Melibee's necessary softness over his daughter's loss and his wife's reac-tions to it. Sophie (i.e., wisdom) is resuscitated just to the level of Prudence's basically avertive genius; Prudence is a moral crea-tive force, a *vertu,* the expert organizer in a field we can call *psychês oikonomikê,* the angel hovering over every plausible fact that may yet make *sophiê* possible again. Prudence's advice for detachment from possessions and for obvious (read shortsighted) action urges that we, too, take to the fields, not to play but to "preye."

> Economics is the tenth city by which we reach the homeland. It treats of kingdoms and honors . . . offices and ranks. It teaches those on their way to the fatherland where, on a scale of merits, human beings stand by comparison to the ranks of the angels.

Selected Bibliography

Because the critical bibliography of Chaucer is quite sizable, only book titles (with one exception) have been listed under the various headings below. The books listed are among the books most frequently used in Chaucer studies today, and their listing here also betokens the indebtedness of this book's contributors to them. This "Selected Bibliography," however, does not include all of the critical and scholarly works that have been cited in the preceding essays.

EDITIONS

Baugh, A. C., ed. *Chaucer's Major Poetry*. New York: Appleton-Century-Crofts, 1963.

Donaldson, E. Talbot, ed. *Chaucer's Poetry: An Anthology for the Modern Reader*. New York: Ronald Press, 1958.

Pratt, Robert A., ed. *The Tales of Canterbury*. Boston: Houghton Mifflin, 1974.

Robinson, F. N., ed. *The Works of Geoffrey Chaucer,* 2d ed. Boston: Houghton Mifflin, 1957. This is the definitive edition.

SOURCES AND ANALOGUES

Benson, Larry, D. and Theodore M. Andersson, eds. *The Literary Context of Chaucer's Fabliaux*. Indianapolis and New York: Bobbs-Merrill, 1971.

Bryan, W. F. and Germaine Dempster, eds. *Sources and Analogues of Chaucer's Canterbury Tales*. New York: The Humanities Press, 1958.

BIBLIOGRAPHIES AND HANDBOOKS

Baugh, A. C. *Chaucer*. Goldentree Bibliographies. New York: Appleton-Century-Crofts, 1968.

Crawford, William R. *Bibliography of Chaucer 1954–63*. Seattle and London: University of Washington Press, 1967.

French, Robert Dudley. *A Chaucer Handbook,* 2d ed. New York: F. S. Crofts, 1947.

Griffith, Dudley D. *Bibliography of Chaucer 1908–53*. Seattle: University of Washington Press, 1955.

Rowland, Beryl, ed. *Companion to Chaucer Studies*. Toronto/New York/London: Oxford University Press, 1968.

REFERENCE WORKS

Magoun, Francis P., Jr. *A Chaucer Gazeteer*. Chicago: University of Chicago Press; and Uppsala: Almqvist & Wiksell, 1961.

Ross, Thomas W. *Chaucer's Bawdy*. New York: Dutton, 1972.

Tatlock, John S. P. and A. G. Kennedy. *Concordance to the Complete Works of Geoffrey Chaucer and to the Romaunt of the Rose*. Gloucester, Mass.: Peter Smith, 1963.

Whiting, B. J. *Chaucer's Use of Proverbs*. Harvard Studies in Comparative Literature 11. Cambridge, Mass.: Harvard University Press, 1934.

BIOGRAPHICAL WORKS

Brewer, D. S. *Chaucer in His Time*. London: Nelson, 1963.

Chute, Marchette. *Geoffrey Chaucer of England*. New York: Dutton, 1946.

Crow, Martin M. and Clair C. Olson, eds. *Chaucer Life-Records*. Oxford: Clarendon Press; and Austin: University of Texas Press, 1966.

JOURNAL

The Chaucer Review: A Journal of Medieval Studies and Literary Criticism. Pennsylvania State University Press, 1966—.

Each volume contains a valuable annual report on Chaucer research.

COLLECTIONS OF CRITICISM

Benson, Larry D., ed. *The Learned and the Lewed: Studies in Chaucer and Medieval Literature*. Harvard English Studies 5. Cambridge, Mass.: Harvard University Press, 1974.

Brewer, D. S., ed. *Chaucer and Chaucerians: Critical Studies in Middle English Literature*. University, Ala.: University of Alabama Press, 1966.

————, ed. *Writers and their Background: Geoffrey Chaucer*. Athens, Ohio: Ohio University Press, 1975.

Burrow, J. A., ed. *Geoffrey Chaucer*. Penguin Critical Anthologies. Baltimore: Penguin Books, 1969.

Cawley, A. C., ed. *Chaucer's Mind and Art*. New York: Barnes & Noble, 1970.

Mitchell, Jerome and William Provost, eds. *Chaucer the Love Poet*. Athens, Ga.: University of Georgia Press, 1973.

Newstead, Helaine, ed. *Chaucer and His Contemporaries*. New York: Fawcett, 1968.

Owen, Charles A., Jr., ed. *Discussions of the Canterbury Tales*. Boston: Heath, 1962.

Schoeck, Richard and Jerome Taylor, eds. *Chaucer Criticism*, 2 vols.: vol. 1, *The Canterbury Tales;* vol. 2, *Troilus and Criseyde and Minor Poems*. Notre Dame, Ind.: University of Notre Dame Press, 1960, 1961.

Wagenknecht, Edward, ed. *Chaucer: Modern Essays in Criticism*. New York: Oxford University Press, 1959.

BOOKS ABOUT CHAUCER'S POETRY

Bennett, H. S. *Chaucer and the Fifteenth Century*. Oxford History of English Literature. Oxford: Oxford University Press, 1947.

Bloomfield, Morton W. *Essays and Explorations: Studies in Ideas, Language, and Literature*. Cambridge, Mass.: Harvard University Press, 1970. Contains essays on Chaucer.

Bowden, Muriel. *A Commentary on the General Prologue to the Canterbury Tales*. New York: Macmillan, 1948.

————. *A Reader's Guide to Geoffrey Chaucer*. New York: Farrar, Straus, 1964.

Curry, Walter Clyde. *Chaucer and the Mediaeval Sciences,* 2d ed. New York: Barnes & Noble, 1960.

Dempster, Germaine. *Dramatic Irony in Chaucer*. Stanford University Publications in Language and Literature 4, no. 3, 1932. New York: The Humanities Press, 1959.

Donaldson, E. Talbot. *Speaking of Chaucer*. New York: Norton, 1972.

Everett, Dorothy. *Essays on Middle English Literature*. Edited by Patricia Kean. Oxford: Clarendon Press, 1955. Contains essays on Chaucer.

Huppé, Bernard F. *A Reading of the Canterbury Tales*. Albany, N.Y.: State University of New York Press, 1964.

Hussey, Maurice, A. C. Spearing, and James Winny. *An Introduction to Chaucer*. Cambridge: at the University Press, 1965.

Jordan, Robert M. *Chaucer and the Shape of Creation: The Aesthetic Possibilities of Inorganic Structure*. Cambridge, Mass.: Harvard University Press, 1967.

Kellogg, Alfred L. *Chaucer, Langland, Arthur: Essays in Middle English Literature*. New Brunswick, N.J.: Rutgers University Press, 1972.

Kittredge, George Lyman. *Chaucer and His Poetry*. Cambridge, Mass.: Harvard University Press, 1956, first published 1915.

Lawrence, William W. *Chaucer and the Canterbury Tales*. New York: Columbia University Press, 1950.

Lowes, John J. *Geoffrey Chaucer*. Bloomington, Ind.: Indiana University Press, 1958.

Lumiansky, Robert M. *Of Sundry Folk: The Dramatic Principle in the Canterbury Tales*. Austin: University of Texas Press, 1955.

Manly, John M. *Some New Light on Chaucer*. New York, Holt, 1926.

Mann, Jill *Chaucer and Medieval Estates Satire: The Literature of the Social Classes and the General Prologue to the Canterbury Tales*. Cambridge: at the University Press, 1973.

Muscatine, Charles. *Chaucer and the French Tradition: A Study in Style and Meaning*. Berkeley and Los Angeles: University of California Press, 1957.

Patch, Howard R. *On Rereading Chaucer*. Cambridge, Mass.: Harvard University Press, 1939.

Payne, Robert O. *The Key of Remembrance: A Study of*

Chaucer's Poetics. New Haven and London: Yale University Press for the University of Cincinnati, 1963.

Robertson, D. W., Jr. *A Preface to Chaucer: Studies in Medieval Perspectives.* Princeton, N.J. Princeton University Press, 1962.

Root, Robert K. *The Poetry of Chaucer,* 2d ed. Gloucester, Mass.: Peter Smith, 1957.

Ruggiers, Paul G. *The Art of the Canterbury Tales.* Madison and Milwaukee: University of Wisconsin Press, 1965.

Whittock, Trevor. *A Reading of the Canterbury Tales.* Cambridge: at the University Press, 1970.

Wood, Chauncey. *Chaucer and the Country of the Stars: Poetic Uses of Astrological Imagery.* Princeton, N.J.: Princeton University Press, 1970.

BOOKS ABOUT CHAUCER AND HIS CONTEMPORARIES

Benson, Larry D. *Art and Tradition in Sir Gawain and the Green Knight.* New Brunswick, N.J.: Rutgers University Press, 1965.

Bloomfield, Morton W. *Piers Plowman as a Fourteenth Century Apocalypse.* New Brunswick, N.J.: Rutgers University Press, 1961.

Borroff, Marie. *Sir Gawain and the Green Knight: A Stylistic and Metrical Study.* New Haven: Yale University Press, 1962.

Burrow, J. A. *Ricardian Poetry.* New Haven: Yale University Press, 1971.

Ford, Boris, ed. *The Age of Chaucer.* The Pelican Guide to English Literature, vol. 1, rev. ed. Baltimore: Penguin Books, 1969.

Howard, Donald R. *The Three Temptations: Medieval Man in Search of the World.* Princeton, N.J.: Princeton University Press, 1966.

Kirk, Elizabeth D. *The Dream Thought of Piers Plowman.* New Haven: Yale University Press, 1972.

Lawlor, John, ed. *Patterns of Love and Courtesy.* Evanston, Ill. Northwestern University Press, 1966.

Muscatine, Charles. *Poetry and Crisis in the Age of Chaucer.* Notre Dame and London: University of Notre Dame Press, 1972.

RECOMMENDED BACKGROUND BOOKS

Allen, Judson Boyce. *The Friar as Critic: Literary Attitudes in the Later Middle Ages*. Nashville, Tenn. Vanderbilt University Press, 1971.

Curtius, E. R. *European Literature and the Latin Middle Ages*. Translated by Willard R. Trask. New York: Pantheon Books, 1953.

Ferrante, Joan M. and George D. Economou, eds. *In Pursuit of Perfection: Courtly Love in Medieval Literature*. Port Washington, N.Y. and London: National University Publications, Kennikat Press, 1975.

Hauser, Arnold. *The Social History of Art,* vol. 1. Translated by the author and Stanley Godman. New York: Vintage, 1951.

Hussey, Maurice. *Chaucer's World: A Pictorial Guide*. Cambridge: at the University Press, 1967.

Jackson, W. T. H. *The Literature of the Middle Ages*. New York: Columbia University Press, 1960.

Lewis, C. S. *The Allegory of Love*. London: Oxford University Press, 1936.

————. *The Discarded Image: An Introduction to Medieval and Renaissance Literature*. Cambridge: at the University Press, 1964.

Loomis, Roger S. *A Mirror of Chaucer's World*. Princeton, N.J.: Princeton University Press, 1965.

Newman, F. X., ed. *The Meaning of Courtly Love*. Albany, N.Y.: State University of New York Press, 1968.

Rickert, Edith. *Chaucer's World*. Edited by C. C. Olson and M. Crow. New York: Columbia University Press, 1948.

Robertson, D. W., Jr. *Chaucer's London*. New York/London/Sydney/Toronto: John Wiley & Sons, 1968.

Southern, R. W. *The Making of the Middle Ages*. New Haven: Yale University Press, 1953.

Wetherbee, Winthrop. *Platonism and Poetry in the Twelfth Century: The Literary Influence of the School of Chartres*. Princeton, N.J.: Princeton University Press, 1972.